THE

RULES
OF MONEY

How to Make It and
How to Hold on to It

RICHARD TEMPLAR

FT Press

FINANCIAL TIMES

Upper Saddle River, NJ • Boston • Indianapolis • San Francisco
New York • Toronto • Montreal • London • Munich • Paris • Madrid
Cape Town • Sydney • Tokyo • Singapore • Mexico City

Vice President, Publisher: Tim Moore
Acquisitions Editor: Martha Cooley
Editorial Assistant: Pamela Boland
Development Editor: Russ Hall
Associate Editor-in-Chief and Director of Marketing: Amy Neidlinger
Publicist: Amy Fandrei
Marketing Coordinator: Megan Colvin
Cover Designer: Sandra Schroeder
Managing Editor: Gina Kanouse
Senior Project Editor: Lori Lyons
Copy Editor: Karen Gill
Compositor: Jake McFarland
Manufacturing Buyer: Dan Uhrig

© 2007 by Pearson Education, Inc.
Publishing as FT Press
Upper Saddle River, New Jersey 07458

FT Press offers excellent discounts on this book when ordered in quantity for bulk purchases or special sales. For more information, please contact U.S. Corporate and Government Sales, 1-800-382-3419, corpsales@pearsontechgroup.com. For sales outside the U.S., please contact International Sales at international@pearsoned.com.

Printed in the United States of America

First Printing February 2007

ISBN 0-13-239410-3

Pearson Education LTD.
Pearson Education Australia PTY, Limited.
Pearson Education Singapore, Pte. Ltd.
Pearson Education North Asia, Ltd.
Pearson Education Canada, Ltd.
Pearson Educatión de Mexico, S.A. de C.V.
Pearson Education—Japan
Pearson Education Malaysia, Pte. Ltd.

Contents

Part II: Getting Wealthy   43

Acknowledgments

I would like to thank Dan Clayden, director of Clayden Associates—
Independent Financial Advisers (www.claydenassociates.co.uk),
who was so kind as to go through a draft of this book in the early
stages and put me right on a few things. He is one of the best
financial advisers I have ever met professionally.

I would also like to dedicate this book to my delightful father-in-
law, who manages his money in a kind, generous, honest, and
moral way and still manages to make it work for him efficiently
and expertly. He is an example to all of us. He is a Rules Player
par excellence.

Introduction

Let's be honest. We all want to be well off, wealthy, rich, abundant. And we're fascinated by others who already are. How did they do it? How can we do it, too?

The simple truth is that wealthy people tend to understand and do things the rest of us don't. From mindsets to actual actions, they follow behavioral rules when it comes to their wealth, and these rules are what separate them from everybody else. This book codifies what those behaviors are so that you, too, can choose to be more wealthy. The basis of the Rules (as with the other Rules books) is that these are all things I have observed wealthy people do. This is, if you like, sympathetic magic. If we do like them, we'll become like them. This actually does work.

Quite simply, this book reveals

- What people do to make money
- How they carry on making money
- How they hang onto it once they've got it
- How they spend it
- How they invest it
- How they enjoy it
- How they make use of it altruistically

In all probability, you'd want to do as little as possible to get to be wealthy, rich, and abundant. A staggering $80 billion is gambled in the U.S.[1] each year. Gambling levels of $80 billion means there are a lot of people looking for an easy way to make some

---

[1] American Gaming Association: Fact Sheets. http://www.americangaming.org/Industry/factsheets/statistics_detail.cfv?id=7.

money. Gambling $80 billion also means a lot of them are going to be disappointed. Not all of them, mind you. Casinos work on percentages—just like any business. Roulette, for instance, if the game is run properly, runs on about 28 percent. That means if $100 crosses the table, the house expects to pocket $28 of that. It returns $72 to the players—not necessarily the same ones who staked it. Some will lose. Some will win. And some will break even. But the house will always, always win—in the long term. That's a fact.

Now, if so many people are gambling so much, it implies to me—and I did notice this a lot when I worked in a casino—that they

- Have too much spare cash and need to get rid of some of it[2]
- Firmly believe in their own "luckiness"
- Like to lose so they can have a reason to feel wretched
- Are desperate for easy money

This book is not for people who are after any or all of the above. No, not even the easy money bit (sorry). However, it should make a significant improvement to your overall prosperity.

This book provides a set of principles, strategies, and things to understand and to do that won't make you get rich quick, but they will increase the odds of your making money and growing your wealth while remaining a decent person. In effect, you can become the house and always win. So, what do you have to do?

Well, there are a number of things you can do. No individual rule guarantees success. But each narrows the odds. They all increase your chances of making money. It's not as easy as a quick win on the blackjack table, but it is more assured and long term, and it doesn't make you an addict or have you chasing a losing streak.

---

[2] Some of them are there to launder money—put spare cash across the tables and then not play but get it back in the form of a winner's check, so they don't have to pay tax on it. Very naughty. Trouble is the house invariably takes its 28 percent off them as well no matter how hard they try to get out without playing much.

No need for violins here, but I was poor as a kid. I went without. I knew others had more, had lots. I also knew, really, really knew, that I would work my way out of that poor upbringing. But it took a lot of false starts, a whole lot of nearly made-its, before I got it right. And I only got it right when I took the time and trouble to observe what the really rich do. That knowledge, based on those observations, I now happily pass on to you.

I'm going to assume you want to

- Get richer
- Do it legally
- Do something useful with it once you've got it
- Put something back
- Keep some of this stuff under your hat

and that you are prepared to put in a bit of work.

To help you achieve this, I have divided this book into five sections:

- Thinking wealthy
- Getting wealthy
- Getting even wealthier
- Staying wealthy
- Sharing your wealth

We start with thinking wealthy because that's the foundation on which all things wealth-related rest. We all have money beliefs. Most of us believe that even if money doesn't make us happy (but secretly, of course, we believe it will), it will at least allow us to be miserable in some comfort. We almost all believe that money lets us buy better stuff, and by buying better stuff, we will be happier. It's not for me to discourage you in any of those beliefs, merely to give you means of finding out for yourself whether or not this is true.

Time to start. Shall we begin? Whatever happens, here's to your greater prosperity.

Richard Templar

PART I

THINKING
WEALTHY

Money is a concept. You can't really see or touch it (unless you are holding a gold bar in your hand). You can only do that with some physical symbol of it like paper currency or a check. They're bits of paper, yes, but bits of paper with enormous power.

The concept of money comes with a lot of baggage to most of us. We have an inherent belief that it is good or bad and that wanting it is good or bad. That loving it is good or bad. That spending it is good or bad.

What I am going to suggest in the first few Rules is that maybe, just maybe, how we think about wealth might be holding us back from having wealth. If, in our heart, we believe (even subconsciously) that money is a bad thing and having lots and lots of it is a really bad thing, then chances are we might be undermining our own efforts, unwittingly, to get lots of it.

I am also going to get you to look at how much effort you are prepared to put into making money. It's a bit like a sport—the more you practice, the better you become. Likewise, you can't make money while being lazy. You've got to put in some work here, you know.

You've also got to know pretty intimately what you want, why you want it, how you think you are going to get it, what you are going to do with it after you've got it—stuff like that. No one said this was going to be easy.

Anybody Can Make Money—It Isn't Selective or Discriminatory

The lovely thing about money is that it really doesn't discriminate. It doesn't care what color or race you are, what class you are, what your parents did, or even who you *think* you are. Each and every day starts with a clean slate so that no matter what you did yesterday, today begins anew, and you have the same rights and opportunities as everyone else to take as much as you want. The only thing that can hold you back is yourself and your own money myths (*see Rule 5*).

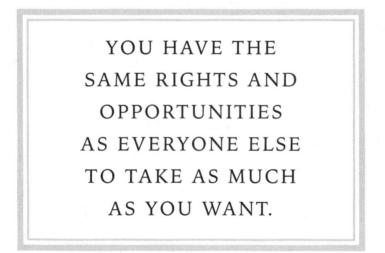

YOU HAVE THE SAME RIGHTS AND OPPORTUNITIES AS EVERYONE ELSE TO TAKE AS MUCH AS YOU WANT.

Of the wealth of the world, each has as much as he takes. What else could make sense? There is no way money can know who is handling it, what his qualifications are, what ambitions he has, or what class he belongs to. Money has no ears, eyes, or senses. It is inert, inanimate, impassive. It hasn't a clue. It is there to be used and spent, saved and invested, fought over, seduced with, and worked for. It has no discriminatory apparatus, so it can't judge whether you are "worthy" or not.

I have watched a lot of extremely wealthy people, and the one thing they all have in common is that they have nothing in common—apart from all being Rules Players, of course. The wealthy are a diverse band of people—the least likely can be loaded. They vary from the genteel to the uncouth, the savvy to the plain stupid, the deserving to the undeserving. But each and every one of them has stepped up and said, "Yes please, I want some of that." And the poor are the ones saying, "No thank you. Not for me. I am not worthy. I am not deserving enough. I couldn't. I mustn't. I shouldn't."

That's what this book is about—challenging your perceptions of money and the wealthy. We all assume the poor are poor because of circumstances, their background, their upbringing, and their nurture. But if you have the means to buy a book such as this and live in comparative security and comfort in the world, then you, too, have the power to be wealthy. It may be hard. It may be tough. But it is doable. And that is Rule 1— anyone can be wealthy; you just have to apply yourself. All the other Rules are about that application.

RULE 2

Decide on Your Definition of Wealth

So, what, to *you*, is wealth? This is one you have to sit down and work out in advance if you are going to get wealthy. My observation is that wealthy people invariably have worked this one out. They know exactly what, to them, wealth means.

I have a wealthy and extremely generous friend who says that he knew long ago when he was starting out in business that he would consider he had made enough when he wasn't living off the money he had amassed (which we will call his capital). Nor would he be living off the interest on his capital. No, he would consider himself wealthy when he was living on the interest on the interest on his capital. Sounds good to me.

Now, this friend knows how much his interest on the interest is making him, pretty much by the hour. Thus, if we all go out for a meal in the evening, he knows (a) how much the meal has cost and (b) how much he has made while eating the meal. He says that as long as (b) is more than (a), he is happy.

This is setting the definition of wealth pretty high, you might think. Maybe you wouldn't want to set it this high. And that's fine, of course. Then again, maybe you'd want to put some kind of figure on it. In the old days, everyone wanted to be a millionaire. That was an easy one to judge if you'd gotten there or not. Today, there are a lot of people who have houses worth more than that, and they wouldn't consider themselves wealthy at all and yet haven't quite gotten around to upping the ante to wishing themselves billionaires.[3]

---

[3] Sorry, but to me a billion is a million million, and I won't be persuaded otherwise.

My own definition, for comparison, is having enough so that I don't have to worry about having enough. How much is that? I never know. There always seems to be more to worry about—and less coming in. But seriously, I feel that I have been "comfortable" since I started counting in thousands of dollars rather than in ones. I know to the nearest thousand how much I've got, how much I need, and how much I can spend.

For some people, not worrying might mean having enough to pay for any emergency that might arise in their family or home. So how will you define it? By the number of cars you own? Servants? Cash in the bank? Value of your house? Portfolio of investments? There are, of course, no right or wrong answers, but I do feel that until you've worked this one out, you shouldn't read on. If we don't have a target, we can't take aim. If we don't have a destination, we can't leave home, or we'll be driving around in circles for hours. If we don't have a definition, how can we monitor or judge success? If we don't do this, how will you know if this book has been helpful to you?

> # IF WE DON'T HAVE A DEFINITION, HOW CAN WE MONITOR OR JUDGE SUCCESS? IF WE DON'T DO THIS, HOW WILL YOU KNOW IF THIS BOOK HAS BEEN HELPFUL TO YOU?

Set Your Objectives

By defining what you mean by wealth, you now have a destination. Setting your objectives is establishing a timetable to reach that destination. It's quite simple. If you know you are going to drive to a certain place, it makes sense to know

- What time you are leaving home
- What time you expect to arrive
- What route you are going to take
- What you will be doing when you get there

Getting rich is the same. You will want to know in advance what rich means to you, how you intend to get there, how long you expect it to take, and what you are going to be able to do or want to do with your money when you get it.

So, having defined what wealth means to you, can you now see the importance of setting your objective? Think about how you intend to get rich and how long it is going to take you, and then set your objective. It might be simple: "I am going to be a millionaire by my fortieth birthday, and I shall make my money by running my own property development company."

That was easy. Well, it was for me, because I'm only making up an example for you. For you, I wager it's going to be pretty hard. This is because you won't have thought about this before. Oh, I daresay you might have had a casual dream—I want to be very, very rich and/or famous and/or successful. But few people—only the rich, famous, and successful ones in my observation—actually decide what and when and how. You have to define wealth if you, too, want to be wealthy. And I assume you do, or you wouldn't be reading this far. Good for you.

Now set your objective. I can wait.

Back already? How did you do? Your objective has to be realistic, honest, and achievable. By realistic, I mean that setting an objective of being the richest person in the world might happen, but it isn't going to. It isn't realistic.

Honest means you have to be true to yourself and set an objective that you can live with and work with. Lying to yourself means your objective will fail. Lying to others means it will fail.

Achievable? Yes, that too. If you know nothing about property and aren't interested in learning, have no capital, and can't get a mortgage, setting an objective to be a property developer isn't realistic, honest, or achievable.

Happy with what you've got? Good. If not, try it again, and let's move on. I want to get you up and running as soon as possible.

> # YOU WILL WANT TO KNOW IN ADVANCE WHAT RICH MEANS TO YOU, HOW YOU INTEND TO GET THERE, AND HOW LONG YOU EXPECT IT TO TAKE.

Keep It Under Your Hat

Now that you have embarked on a new journey, a new direction, it might be worth keeping it under your hat. There may come a time when you will need to discuss what you are doing with money mentors (*see Rule 64*) but, for the moment, don't broadcast what you are doing. There are several reasons for this:

- Other people's opinions can often be negative, and this can put you off.
- If everyone is doing it, there may be less room for you.
- There's no need to give away all your best ideas.
- Having other people discussing your business among themselves is never good for you.
- You don't want to be seen as preaching or trying to convert people to your way of thinking.
- No one else really wants to know what you're up to. If someone asks how you are, reply with a simple "Fine" rather than a lengthy explanation of what you are doing.
- It's nice having a secret. It gives you a warm, smug, glowing feeling.

If you go around broadcasting what you're doing, there will be people around you who will get jealous and will do almost anything to put you off. After all, you are saying goodbye to them in a way. You are proclaiming that the old you, the old lifestyle, isn't good enough any more, and you are off to new pastures. Of course, people are going to be unhappy about that. So keep it under your hat. That doesn't cost anything or require you to do anything.

RULE 4

> NOW THAT YOU HAVE
> EMBARKED ON A NEW
> JOURNEY, A NEW
> DIRECTION, IT MIGHT
> BE WORTH KEEPING
> IT UNDER YOUR HAT.

Let this be our little secret. Carry on learning and practicing the Rules, but just don't go telling all—no matter how much you think they might benefit from reading this book. Leave a copy around by all means, of course.

The interesting bit is that even if you did go telling all your friends, they would be unlikely to do anything about it. Most people would rather watch television than drag themselves out of their pit of poverty. I am thinking only of you when I say keep it under your hat. Anyone who gets religion of any sort needs to keep a tight lid on it. People really hate being preached at, lectured at, encouraged to think about their lifestyle, or told that what they are doing isn't good enough. Gaining prosperity is one of those things you do privately, clandestinely, surreptitiously. It's not that there is anything wrong. It's just that it's best done alone.

Most People Are Too Lazy to Be Wealthy

You have to get up early, work hard all day, and go to bed still working on your objective. Yes, money *does* sometimes grow on trees—or so it seems. Yes, people *do* win the lottery, the jackpot, the big prize. People *do* get sudden inheritances from long-lost relatives. Yes, people *do* suddenly find fame and fortune where they sought for none. But it isn't going to happen to you. Well, the odds are that it won't. If you set your objective as, **Win the lottery and live in the lap of luxury forevermore,** then read no further. Put this book down, and go and buy lottery tickets. If your objective is a little more realistic, read on.

Most people are too lazy to be rich. They may say they want to be rich, but they don't. They may buy a lottery ticket as a sort of half-hearted gesture of wanting to be rich, but they aren't prepared to put in the work. They aren't prepared to make sacrifices, study, learn, work their socks off, put in the effort, and make it a determined and concentrated focus of their life.

And for a lot of them—not you—it is because they believe that if they want to become rich and work hard to do so, they are somehow tainted with evil (*see Rule 6*). But is it okay to work hard to make money? Is it a worthwhile thing to want? It depends on why and what you are going to do with it, I guess (*see Rule 8*).

Most people don't want to do the work. Yes, they want the money, but only if it comes to them by accident, by luck, or by chance. Then it's okay. Then it's not tainted with sweat and work and passion and focus.

> # MOST PEOPLE ARE TOO LAZY TO BE RICH. THEY MAY SAY THEY WANT TO BE RICH, BUT THEY DON'T.

I think if you look at anyone rich enough to be a role model— Bill Gates, Richard Branson, Alan Sugar, Warren Buffett, Gordon Ramsey, James Dyson, Petr Kellner[1]—you'll notice only one thing in common—they work their socks off. They might make their money from computers, sales, cookery, business, the film industry, vacuum cleaners, pop music, radio stations, whatever. But the one thing they all share is the ability to do more in a day than most of us do in a month.

That's the wonderful thing about wealth—it's lying around waiting to be claimed (*remember Rule 1*). Those who claim it are the ones who get up early, work hard, and put in the hours.

And you are going to have to as well. I don't have loafers, weight shifters, or decorative spongers on my team. I want hard-working, dedicated, focused, ambitious, driven moneymakers. With a sense of fun, of course.

---

[4] I did have a bet with myself that you wouldn't have heard of him—the Czech Republic's first billionaire.

Understand Your Money Beliefs and Where They Come From

We all grow up with money myths. We get a lot of them from our parents and the way they bring us up. I can still hear my mother saying, "A penny saved is a penny found," and to this day, I still have no idea what it means. Maybe I'm lucky. My money myths are based on a lot of nonsense like that. But most of us have the following ingrained beliefs:

- Money is the root of all evil.[5]
- Money is dirty.
- I don't deserve to be rich.
- Money is only made by the greedy and dishonest.
- Money corrupts.
- You shouldn't brag about money—never say how much you earn, are worth, or paid for something (unless it is a bargain).
- You can't have money and be "spiritually pure."[6]
- You lose your friends if you get rich.
- You have to work too hard to get rich.[7]
- Happiness and money make poor bedfellows.
- The more you have, the more you'll want.
- It is somehow better to be poor.
- I wasn't meant to be rich—if I were, I would have been by now.
- I'm not the right type to be rich.

---

[5] It is actually the *love* of money that is supposed to be the root of all evil, but is it a belief of yours?

[6] Whatever that means.

[7] See Rule 5.

Have a quick look. Check which ones you believe. Check which ones strike a chord with you. Now you have to do a bit of that old-fashioned hard work. Write down ones that mean something to you. Add ones I've missed—there will be a few. Then work out why you hold these beliefs. Is it something you have actively thought about, reasoned out, dedicated some research to? Or are they inherited, left over, or picked up along the way?

Get rid of any that you can question and accept as nonsense. Discard any that simply aren't true. And chuck out any that stand in the way, hold you back, or stop you from making some money.

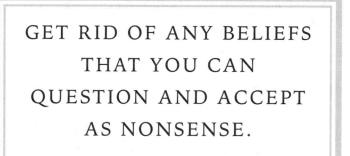

GET RID OF ANY BELIEFS
THAT YOU CAN
QUESTION AND ACCEPT
AS NONSENSE.

What you should be left with is none at all, nothing, a blank sheet. Now you can write new beliefs, such as

- Money is okay.
- Wanting money is okay.
- I am going to be wealthy.
- I am prepared to put in the work.

Wealthy people have none of the troublesome money myths that we poorer people have. They have purged them or never had them. If we, too, purge them, we stand a better chance of getting there.

Understand That Wealth Is a Consequence, Not a Reward[8]

If you work hard at making money, you stand a better chance of becoming rich. You have to accept that money is a payment given to you for clever thinking and hard work. The harder and smarter you work, the more you will earn. You aren't given the money by a committee who examines whether you deserve it or not, whether you have been good enough or not. It is a direct consequence.

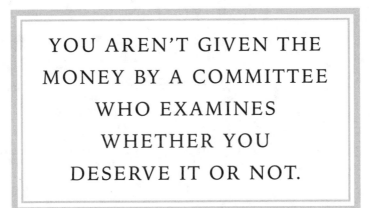

YOU AREN'T GIVEN THE MONEY BY A COMMITTEE WHO EXAMINES WHETHER YOU DESERVE IT OR NOT.

We often look at someone who has money and make all sorts of value judgments about whether they deserve it. We all do it. I was reading about Calvin Ayre, the Internet bookie from the UK who has grown very rich running online gambling. He has

---

[8] I use the word "reward" in the sense of a prize or bonus, not as a payment or renumeration.

something like 16 million customers in the United States. The U.S. Department of Justice isn't very happy about this and wants to shut him down. You can read all about him on the www.Forbes.com website (home of the really wealthy folk). If it isn't your home page, it ought to be. You are in this to be wealthy, which means understanding where wealth comes from.

Back to Ayres. He has grown rich exploiting an alleged U.S. law loophole whereby what he does is alleged to be illegal, but he isn't in the country to commit any crime. Do we judge him? I don't. I study this information to see if I could make use of it. What might be wrong is the gambling. But I am aware that his consequence of hard work has been lots of money.

I was watching a TV program the other day about a man who cleans and polishes cars for rich celebs. He charges $10,000 for car washing. Mind you, this does include polishing. Now, is his money a reward or a consequence? I don't think he would see it as a reward. It's the price he sets, and customers pay him because he is the best car cleaner in the world. The consequence of his business idea, skill, and effort are to be very well paid.

See Wealth as a Friend, Not the Enemy

Writing this book has made me question my own attitudes toward money in a big way. And it was an interesting process to go through.

We all have to handle money. We all have bank accounts and credit cards and loans and overdrafts and mortgages. We all deal with the paraphernalia of money every day of our lives. We all need/want more. So what's the problem?

It's all about what goes on in our heads. Like you, I handle money, spend money, and save money. And I want to do so more efficiently, more happily.

So before I could write this for you, I had to undergo a rigorous investigation of my own motives, myths, and inherent stuff. And I came to accept that money is neither good nor bad, neither friend nor foe. It is not the evil we have come to believe. Without it, life disintegrates. Money is the oil that smooths life for all of us. What we do with it—*see next Rule*—is the good or bad, the right or wrong, the friend or foe.

> ## MONEY IS THE OIL THAT SMOOTHS LIFE FOR ALL OF US.

RULE 8

Repeat after me: *Money is fine. Money is great. Money is necessary. Money is okay. Money is my friend, not my enemy.* Repeat this under your breath, of course, or your family and friends will think you've gone nuts. Learn not to fight money or be embarrassed about having it when you do.

Finally, having money, working toward getting wealthy, doesn't mean you have to change your politics at all. You can be left-wing—radical even—if you want. One of the richest men in Britain is a Labor minister (Lord Sainsbury). Having money won't detract from that at all. Having money won't lessen your spiritual virtues or your karmic harmonics or affect your future incarnations. I promise. What you do with it might, but money is inherently your friend, not foe.

Decide What You Want Money For

This is part of your defining, setting an objective process. There are no right or wrong answers. For example, making a fortune and spending it all on cocaine seems, to me, like a foolish thing to do. But that's personal. You might find a problem with me spending mine on a decent *Châteauneuf du Pape*. We all spend on what we think will satisfy us, make us happy. We all choose our own pleasures, and it's not for me to sit in judgment on anyone else.

So, what do you want the money for? Why do you want to be wealthy? The answers you give will tell you a whole lot about your hidden money myths and how you really see money.

> ## WE ALL SPEND ON WHAT WE THINK WILL SATISFY US, MAKE US HAPPY.

Sometimes, it's very simple: We have a dream and need the money to fulfill it. The dream comes first. Gerald Durrell had wanted a zoo since he was a small boy and wrote 36 bestselling books, which helped to fund his zoo. What's your dream?

It might not be that simple, however. I asked a close acquaintance why she wanted to be wealthier the other day, and the results were quite revealing. She said she wanted to be "better off" so that she could give her children more. And in giving them more, they would stay at home longer. If they stayed at home longer, she wouldn't have to face a possible old age alone. So, basically she wants to be wealthy to stave off loneliness.

Another acquaintance said he wanted to get wealthy so he could have adventures. When pressed further, it seemed his adventures were the "running away" sort where he could be young, free, and single again.

Is money really the answer for either of these people? Is it for you?

When you know what you want greater wealth for, think also about alternative ways to meet your needs: I stated that I wanted to be wealthy so I could pay for medical care for any close family member who might need it. I could invest in some simple medical insurance to cover that instead.

Consider also what you *don't* need more money for. I like my toys—cars and boats—but have found that my investments in such things haven't increased as my income has gone up. I still like old cheap sports cars and old boats that need plenty of maintenance. My motivation isn't to be able to spend loads on new things. I don't need more money to buy new cars and boats. Do you really need as much as you think? If so, fine. You just need to be sure and be clear about it.

So what's your excuse? What do you want money for? Set your own agenda, and keep it to yourself. And whatever you write down—and I do recommend that you write it down because it makes it so much more real—keep it secret, keep it safe. It is a useful exercise to look back on one day and see if your dream and achievements match.

Understand That Money Begets Money

There is no greater truth than this—money makes money. It likes clustering together. It breeds quietly and quickly like rabbits. It prefers to hang out in big groups. Money makes money. The rich get richer; the poor get poorer. That's life. Yes, it is sad. But it does seem to be a fact. Now, we can work hard ourselves and do something about it, or we can sit around moaning and become part of the problem. The choice, as always, is entirely ours.

> ## MONEY MAKES MONEY.
> ## THE RICH GET RICHER.

If you do want to do something about it, it makes sense to earn a tidy sum and use your money wisely to help the less fortunate. Or, do whatever with it you choose.

When you have some money, you'll be astonished at how quickly it can grow. I recommend you understand and learn the concept of *compound interest* as quickly as possible. And no, I am not going to tell you anything about it except it's vitally important that you know about it and make it a cornerstone in your building of wealth. The reason I'm not going to tell you anything about it is that this isn't that sort of a book,[9] and I'm

---

[9] Read *The Financial Times Guide to Investing* by Glen Arnold.

not going to do all the work for you. That would be too easy, and you'd learn nothing. My observation is that wealthy people get the idea of compound interest, and the rest of us don't.

If you spend all you get, this Rule will never work for you; it'll never get your money working for you. You have to set aside money for breeding purposes. If you ran a rabbit farm and killed and ate all your rabbits, you wouldn't have any left to keep going. Forget the rabbit farm—you're going to start a money farm. Your money will breed. You can then reinvest some and spend some—but you can't spend it all, or you'll have no more rabbits. Look, this stuff isn't rocket science, but it is amazing how many people simply don't get it. But you do now. You have been given the best tips I can give you:

- Put some money aside for breeding purposes.
- Cream a little off for spending.
- Reinvest the bulk to build up a good and healthy stock.
- Keep it to yourself.

If You See Money as the Solution, You'll Find It Becomes the Problem

Having money doesn't make all your relationships flow smoothly—not by a long shot. It doesn't protect you from disease—it may buy you better medical care, but it doesn't protect you. It might buy a better diet, but the rich half of the world has a pretty poor health record despite having all the money to feed itself extremely well, so that doesn't necessarily go hand in hand.

> MONEY MAY BUY
> YOU BETTER MEDICAL
> CARE, BUT IT DOESN'T
> PROTECT YOU.

The more you see money as a solution, the greater the chance that you are missing the point entirely. Money doesn't do anything.

I know, I know. You'll be thinking, "If only I had X amount, I could fix this problem in my life." I think you'll find money would throw up a lot more problems in its wake. Money will not make you happier, thinner, or more popular with decent people. Money does not deliver lasting, meaningful peace of mind.

There are plenty of rich, fat, unhappy people with no real friends. I think we need to find the cure to our problems first and then find a way of funding that cure. Money isn't—and never will be—the cure. It is the oil that smooths the wheels. It isn't the engine.

You Can Make Lots of Money, You Can Enjoy Your Job, and You Can Sleep Nights

A lot of people hold one or other—or all—of these notions:

- Making money goes hand in hand with being a ruthless, manipulative, amoral, greedy lizard.
- To make a bit of cash, you have to sell your soul, grandmother, and principles.
- Being wealthy means you end up with a heart problem, insomnia, and other stress-related disorders.
- To make money, you have to turn into a slimeball who sacrifices his family, morals, and happiness—all on the altar of wealth.

Well, it can be like that, but it doesn't have to be. In fact, it shouldn't be. That's the beauty of it. If it *is* like that, then you're doing it wrong. You see, money is so freely available—and to anyone (as we looked at in Rule 1)—that you really don't need to try that hard or change that much. An awful lot of pretty ordinary, nice people make money—and lots of it. The staid old cliché of the cigar-chewing, high-pressure executive barking orders down a phone while signing dodgy deals probably went overboard.

You *can* make money, enjoy your job, and sleep at night. You just have to decide that is what you're going to do—no matter what. And then stick to it.

> ## IF YOU ARE STARTING TO LOSE SLEEP OR HAVE STOPPED ENJOYING WHAT YOU DO, THEN YOU NEED TO HAVE A TALK WITH YOURSELF.

Remember, if you are starting to lose sleep or have stopped enjoying what you do, then you need to have a serious talk with yourself. Go back to the beginning of the book, and remember what it is that wealth is all about to you.

I remember a cartoon of a boardroom with fat-cat executives. A small girl pokes her head round the door and says, "Money can't buy a kind smile." The businessmen all look, momentarily, shamed. Then the chairman growls, "Get outta here, kid, who the hell wants a kind smile?" and the others all look relieved and go back to their meeting.

Well, I for one would like the kind smile even if it does mean I lose a little money. I want to sleep nights and enjoy my job and make money. But I won't compromise my principles, spend too little time with my family or children, neglect to sit in the sunshine occasionally, or take a day off. I won't worry about work or money after I've gone to bed or be driven so much by money that I lose my sense of humor or need to have fun. These I swear by. And it is possible—believe me, I've known and observed enough wealthy people to know this is true—to make money *and* have a life, to be ethical *and* rich, to earn a lot *and* be a thoroughly nice person. It is possible. It just sometimes *seems* it isn't. It's all part of debunking our money myths.

Don't Make Money by Being Bad

I like Google's mission statement—*Don't be evil*. It's probably an anagram of something, but I still like it. If you have to lie, cheat, steal, defraud, lose sleep, hide, dodge the law in any way, break the rules, or generally behave badly to make your money, then don't do it. It isn't worth it.

If earning money or being wealthy stops being fun—and by being bad, it really will stop being fun—then there's no point doing it. If you don't enjoy the challenge of earning money in a decent way, it's best to go and do something different.

I knew a major criminal once. He told me it was no fun being "crooked" because, in fact, he had to be a lot more law-abiding than the rest of us. He couldn't risk getting pulled over by the police for speeding or any minor motoring offence; no late-night parties in case the police got called out; no flashy car to draw attention to himself; and no lavish lifestyle in case it put him in the spotlight.

But there is more to living a clean life than being able to speed or have parties. Living a life where you make your money from being good lets you sleep nights. You get to look your kids in the eye—and yourself in the mirror—with the added bonus of a feel-good factor. No amount of money can buy that.

If you have to resort to being wicked, it means you've failed; you've lost the plot. It means you haven't been able to do it properly. It means you're scraping the barrel. It means you haven't been able to think of a proper idea. It means you've been lazy, desperate, noncreative, and boring.

RULE 13

> ## IF YOU DON'T ENJOY THE CHALLENGE OF EARNING MONEY LEGIT, IT'S BEST TO GO AND DO SOMETHING DIFFERENT.

I can come up with lots of examples of famous wealthy people who made their money out of being bad. Yep, they're wealthy, it's true, but look in their eyes, and what do you see? Do you want to have that stay-awake-at-night-worrying look? Do you want that flinch-when-the-doorbell-rings kind of life? Do you want nobody-trusts-you sort of relationships? Or would you rather relax and know that you did it legitimately, honestly, and fairly? It's a no-brainer really, isn't it?

If you can earn your wealth without ripping people off, being cruel or unjust, breaking the law, or bending the rules, you'll be doing fine. All it requires is a quick check, staying conscious of what you—and your money—are doing.

Money and Happiness— Understand Their Relationship

There are lots of things that will make us miserable—losing a partner, being made redundant, getting sick. And loads more. There are quite a few related to money and gaining or spending.

Remember

- Too little money can make you miserable.
- Too much money can make you miserable.
- Too much stuff can make you miserable.
- Not having enough can make you miserable.

I think what we have to grasp pretty well from Day 1 is that money and happiness are not necessarily the same thing. **Money doesn't buy happiness.** This is a common mistake people make. It isn't going to be one you make. You can be poor and happy. You can be rich and happy. You can also be either poor or rich and miserable.

If you are looking to wealth to make you happy, you'll be disappointed. If you are looking to money to make you more powerful/younger/sexier/more vital/more interesting/better look-ing/whatever, you're going to be disappointed. Sorry, but money doesn't do any of that. In your head, it might. In other people's heads, it might. But it doesn't in reality. You can be all those things with money; it is true. It isn't money that does it. The switch is thrown in your head first. Money is a placebo, not a cure.

We've all seen the lottery winners who buy the big house and feel miserable because they've left all their friends behind. Or the tycoons who lose everything and kill themselves because they felt their life was over just because they were broke.

MONEY IS A PLACEBO, NOT A CURE.

But you won't make any of these mistakes because you will practice this Rule diligently and understand the relationship between money and happiness. Ah, but I hear you ask, "what exactly is this Rule? What do I have to do?" Answer: Nothing except don't expect too much from money, and don't buy stuff in the hope it will make you happy. It won't. When they build that brand new Beemer or whatever it is you covet, they don't build in any happiness. So, when you first sit in it or buy it and you feel fantastic—and I'm not denying people do feel great buying stuff—that feeling isn't in the thing you buy. That feeling was inside you anyway. All this said, what money can do is buy away a lot of _un_happiness. It just can't go any further than that.

Know the Difference between Price and Value

I once asked my delightful father-in-law to explain that thing about wine to me. You know, can a bottle that costs $200 in a top restaurant *really* be twenty times as good as a bottle that you can get for $10 at the local shop?

His answer was interesting. He said that you aren't paying for the wine alone. What you are paying for is the ambience, the service, the location (we're talking Le Cirque or at least Four Seasons here), the wine waiter's expertise, the good company, the fine tablecloths, the privacy and discretion, the style and class, the tradition, the food and the trust, the humidity and storage, the tone and the surroundings, the fellow dining guests, and the great conversation.

The wine is almost an irrelevance, and that's the point. We think we know the price of something. But the value can spread out far beyond all of that.

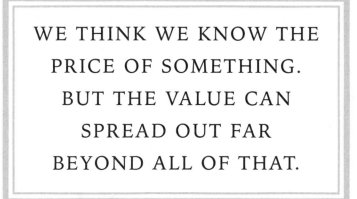

WE THINK WE KNOW THE PRICE OF SOMETHING. BUT THE VALUE CAN SPREAD OUT FAR BEYOND ALL OF THAT.

RULE 15

I have an old Mercedes car. (I like Mercs, but am far too mean to buy a new one and lose all that depreciation.) I didn't pay much for it. You never do, as people are scared of them in case they go wrong. That's fair enough, because they do cost a fortune to put right, *but* you need to remember that because they are better made, they rarely do go wrong. I was visited by a friend who was driving a brand new car he'd just bought. It was a modern import, a small hatchback thing that looked like a mini space-ship. He looked at my old, battered, mud-streaked Merc and exclaimed, "Man, you must be doing well!" I tried to explain that wasn't the case and that he'd probably paid at least five times for his what I'd paid for mine, but he wouldn't have it. He saw the Merc and had decided its value was a lot more than the price— i.e., what was actually paid for it. I learned that day about price not necessarily equating to perceived value.

Remember, too, that something is worth only what others are willing to pay for it. A catalog may say the value of a painting is $1,000, but that's only true if somebody is willing to pay that amount for it. An important lesson to learn. The price of some-thing can be far less than its actual value, either to you or to somebody else. Or a lot more.

If you are going to be wealthy—and I sincerely hope you are, if you put into play the Rules in this book and work diligently at it—then it's worth studying the difference between price and value.

Know How the Wealthy Think

There is a simple test to determine whether someone will end up wealthy—or if he already is. All you have to do is watch someone read his favorite newspaper, especially if it's a big Sunday paper:

- Notice which paper he chooses.
- Notice which sections he chooses to read.
- Notice which sections he discards.
- Notice in which order he reads his chosen sections.

This is a test for you, too. Have a look at the above and make a mental note of what *you* do. The wealthy—those who have deliberately chosen to be wealthy rather than those who have won the lottery or inherited (God's lottery, as I think of it) or married into it—invariably

- Choose the more serious of the papers
- Choose the more serious sections
- Discard the "frivolous" sections
- Read the money/business sections first

If you are serious about being wealthy, you will have to learn how the wealthy think. This means studying the "opposition"— although very shortly you will be a part of them. You need to know the lingo and the language, where they eat and live, how they work and relax, how they invest and save. In short, you need to study money if you are to increase your prosperity. Try to talk to wealthy people. Ask questions. Develop a thirst for understanding and knowledge. Read about wealthy people—interviews and autobiographies can be full of insight.

You may also benefit from a few well-chosen business and finance books. I'm not going to recommend any to you because I don't know your reading style. Just find ones that suit you. Also, why not log on to the *Financial Times* site or the finance pages of other online papers to keep up with the latest developments in the money market. Get informed.

But what if this all feels a bit too heavy? If, like me, you like the gossip columns as well as financial pages, then you, like me, will probably never be extremely, mind-bogglingly over-the-top wealthy. We can still be wealthy—and we might have more fun, too. Prosperous and fun—sounds good to me. I think we have to be really passionate about money if we want lots. We have to live and breathe and sleep (yes, bearing in mind Rule 12) money. We have to study hard at the University of Wealth if we want to graduate.

> ## YOU MAY HAVE TO CHOOSE—MONEY OR FRIVOLITY?

Don't Envy What Others Have

We all set our own objectives. We all have individual ambitions. We all determine how much work we are prepared to put into this business of becoming wealthy. We all set our own limits and know what we are prepared to do or not do. So, what is the point of envying what others have? Not unless you know what their agenda was and is. Not unless you know how much work they were prepared to put in. Not unless you know what they were prepared to sacrifice.

Of course, you can cast an envious glance at the easy three—lottery, inherited, married (or divorced!) into—we all do. But money earned is entirely the business of those earning it. They did the work. They had the idea or entrepreneurial spirit. They got up earlier than us. They were driven or fired up by what they wanted to achieve. Envying them is pointless; learning from them is invaluable.

> ## ENVYING OTHERS IS POINTLESS; LEARNING FROM THEM IS INVALUABLE.

Learning from others is the greatest gift they can give us. Ideally, you need a money mentor. Someone you look up to who has made a lot of money and in the right way—legally, enjoyably, and nicely—who will give you the odd tip, tuck you under his wing, and set you on the right path. And refuse to lend you any money, of course. Not that you'd ask. If I come across someone extremely rich, I immediately try to work out how that person did it and if that route would suit me. What bits of information could I glean to help me get to that position, bearing in mind I only want to do it right—legally and enjoyably?

I think 90 percent of getting these Rules right is to approach getting wealthy as sympathetic magic—do as they do, and you'll end up as them.

I have my money mentor, and I hang on to his every word when it comes to money, as he's living on the interest on the interest on his money—and that's the place I'm heading for.

Use other people as a source of inspiration. Besides, envy is not a characteristic of a Rules Player—that's you now, by the way.

It's Harder to Manage Yourself Than It Is to Manage Your Money

So, how well do you know yourself? Pretty well? Not at all? Vaguely? We think we know ourselves until we try to give up smoking, lose weight, get fit, or get rich. And then we realize we are lazier, have less willpower, have less determination, make less effort, get too easily dissuaded, and fall by the wayside too readily.

If I wanted to tuck you under my wing and make you wealthy, the first thing I would need to know is, "Do you have what it takes to be wealthy? Are you determined enough? Will you work hard enough? Will you stick to it? Do you have backbone? Stamina? Guts? Relentless focus?" You see, if you don't, the chances are you won't succeed. I'm not trying to put you off. I am trying to make you see that making money is a skill that can be taught—if people are ready and willing to learn and apply themselves diligently.

> ## THE FIRST THING I WOULD NEED TO KNOW IS, "DO YOU HAVE WHAT IT TAKES TO BE WEALTHY?"

RULE 18

If you decided you wanted to win Wimbledon, you would have needed to start playing tennis when you were about 5 and have been winning junior championships by the time you were 14. It's the same with money. You can't expect an overweight, middle-aged person to suddenly be in the tennis finals.

When I was a young struggling student, I once sold a valuable book so I could eat. I made a direct choice between owning something that was going to increase in value, and thus potentially make me wealthy, and having a meal. You see what I mean? I, in essence, chose—at that time anyway—to be poor rather than wealthy. I saw the same book recently in a bookshop and, believe me, I made a bad call that day.

What I have noticed is that the wealthy—when they are starting out anyway—have enormous drive and are prepared to make enormous sacrifices. They manage themselves and forego instant rewards for bigger payback in the longer term. Self-control and delayed gratification are useful arts to learn.

PART II

GETTING WEALTHY

We've entered the dark uncharted waters of Part Two. This is where we get serious. This is where we start the real practical stuff. This is where you have to start taking a good hard look at your situation, doing some planning, and taking some action.

Getting wealthy means being very honest with yourself and being willing to invest your time and efforts into the quest for greater prosperity. Many of the Rules are behavioral, and changing your behavior is never easy. Some Rules will seem stunningly simple, but for every Rule you have to ask yourself: "I may already know this—but do I do it?" The willingness to put in the effort and do something, make things happen, is vital.

You've Got to Know Where You Are Before You Start

Before we can go forward, we have to know where we are now. Or rather, *you* have to. When Robinson Crusoe swam ashore from his shipwrecked boat, the first thing he did was check out what supplies, guns, and ammunition he had. Once he knew that, he could assess the situation and move forward.

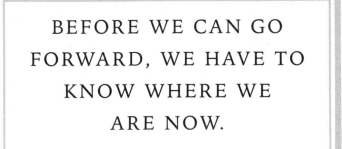

BEFORE WE CAN GO
FORWARD, WE HAVE TO
KNOW WHERE WE
ARE NOW.

So you are going to swim ashore and begin your new life. The first thing you have to do is to take stock. Find out what you've already got, what can be used, what can be discarded or discounted, what you owe, what you are owed, and what basically is your net worth.

We're going to do a full financial audit on you and your life. If you don't know where you are before you start, you can't really work efficiently toward becoming wealthy. It's a wise man who lays out his tools before he begins the job.

All you've got to do is collect all the information—what you owe at the bank (or have in there in your current account, deposit account, savings account), and what you owe on credit cards. Also start working out what you spend on a monthly and annual basis (and where you spend it).

Here's your checklist. It may need adapting to suit your individual circumstances.

Start with the big figures to get a picture of where you are right now overall.

Starting Balance	+	Item	−	Net Worth
		House/mortgage		
		Credit/store cards		
		Bank		
		Savings		
		Pension		
		Loans/overdraft		
		Assets/cars etc.		
		Personal items— jewelry, etc.		
		Investments		
		Debts		

Now that you have an overall figure, you need to look at your typical inflow and outflow of cash on a monthly or annual basis. You can choose which you assess, but all figures have to be made either monthly or annual.

	Item	–	Balance
(Put your salary here)	Fixed regular expenditure (e.g., insurance, bills, food, memberships)		
	Variable regular expenditure (e.g., shopping, holidays)		
	Totals		

This may not be ideal for your circumstances, but I'm sure you get the idea. Don't be tempted to skip this exercise. Even if your financial situation is none too rosy, it's good to face up to reality so that you can take positive action to address the situation.

You've Got to Have a Plan

Why are a fool and his money so easily parted? Because the fool doesn't have a plan. If you don't have a plan, you'll be tempted to fritter your cash away, spend it instead of investing, or forget the new business idea or career move. If you have a plan, you know exactly what does and what doesn't fit into it.

The last Rule helped you work out where you are now, and you already know where you're going (your objective). The plan gives you the important part—how you are going to get there. Back to the Robinson Crusoe analogy. After he had been shipwrecked and taken stock, he made a plan. "I'll need a shelter to keep warm, some food, and something to do." And he set about building a thatched shelter on the beach, which, of course, got blown over in the first gale, and so he had to retreat inland to a cave. You see, even the best plans have to be open to adjustment.

> ## THE PLAN GIVES YOU THE IMPORTANT PART— HOW YOU ARE GOING TO GET THERE.

RULE 20

First things first. If you have a job you love and are happy, then you'll probably want to stick with it. If it doesn't make you enough money, you need a plan to generate income another way. If your job is making you miserable and, what's worse, keeping you in a poverty trap, you must prioritize getting out of it in your plan.

Your plan should involve taking financial control of your life. If you have debts, it will definitely include tackling these as a priority. Ditto about spending excesses. The plan might involve a career change, investigating a business idea, investing money, or generating some capital so that you can enter the market. It may well include selling things. A lot of money is generated through selling things—whether it's a product, a service, or your time and skill. That's why I like writing books—even while I sleep, there is a bookshop somewhere that is selling books for me. In fact, one of the fundamental truths about gettng rich is that wealth—*real* wealth—comes from doing deals, not from earning wages, salaries, or fees.

As General Patton said, "A good plan today is better than a perfect plan tomorrow." Whatever the plan includes, just make sure you have one and that you stick to it. Don't worry. The rest of this book will give you lots of ideas as to what your plan could contain. Just remember: Never sit back and wait for somebody to give you money—ever.

Get Your Finances under Control

In some states, there are river authorities that manage series of flood control dams that also generate power when water passes through the dams. In times of drought, residential homeowners often are put on schedules or even cut off altogether from watering their lawns. They say, "Hey, we see lakes in the river chain. There's water there. Why take it out on us and punish us unfairly? It's up to you to maintain the system and keep water available to us. Maybe it's your antiquated pipe systems that need repair to keep so much water from leaking away uselessly." See where I'm going with this?

You may well have enough money, but it leaks away before you get to spend it, in a whole variety of ways—taxation, paying interest, lack of use (not invested properly), or too much being spent on the wrong things. Before you can control your finances, you have to stop the leaks.

> BEFORE YOU CAN CONTROL YOUR FINANCES, YOU HAVE TO STOP THE LEAKS.

RULE 21

If you carried out the exercise in Rule 19 (of course, you did), you'll have a record of your credit card balances. Higher than you cared to admit? Probably. We are all encouraged to spend on plastic. We are all seduced into racking up debts monthly. If you want to stop the leaks, cut up all the cards and pay them off.[10]

Do a quick calculation and see what levels of interest you are paying. It's the same with your mortgage. Make sure you're not paying more than you have to through negligence. If your fixed rate deal has come to an end, it could be time to check out the best deals that are now available.

Keep a record of everything you spend. *Everything*. Do this for a short while—even just a week—and see where the leakages are. If you are going to be wealthy, first you have to know where your money is going. Sorry if you thought this was going to be easy or this book was going to be full of get-rich-quick schemes. But stick with me, and you'll be glad you did.

When you carry out your financial stock-check, watch out for the hidden things that you can easily overlook, such as direct debits and subscriptions that are too high, wrong, or out of date. The rich are eagle-eyed and miss nothing.

---

[10] And spend what? I hear you ask. Spend what you can afford on what you have to, and above that, spend nothing for a while. Make the choice: wealth or spending sprees. You've tried the spending sprees. We all have. Now take the prosperity route and see if it isn't better. You are only postponing spending, not cancelling it forever. You'll also be able to spend more later. Look forward to that as you tighten your belt. Think of the better belt you'll be able to buy.

Only by Looking Wealthy Can You Become Wealthy

I once watched a man looking at a job vacancy board. He was dressed in a scruffy sweatsuit, wore the hood (up), was unshaven, and slouched with his hands in his pockets. You just knew he was going to go for job interviews dressed like that—and fail to get them. And then he'd claim it was unfair, nobody would give him a break, life sucks, and so on.

I've held many job interviews and have always been seriously underimpressed with the way people turned up. The lack of effort is always staggering—as is the lack of research and interest. "Why do you want to work for this company?" "Dunno." "What do we do here?" "Dunno."

I'm trying not to be an old reactionary here. But I can't fail to notice that the lack of effort is directly related to the lack of results. The poor look poor. Not because they have to. They wear a uniform that makes them stand out. If they change that uniform, they change their circumstances, because people will react differently to them. We aren't too far removed from the great apes, and they relate to each other based a lot on how they move and look. Those who look weak and needy are treated as such. The powerful will strut and look confident. What I am suggesting is that you need to look powerful and confident. We should all look powerful and confident.

> # YOU NEED TO LOOK POWERFUL AND CONFIDENT.

Ah, but how can we afford to dress as if we are more wealthy? Come on, come on. I expected better of you. Think laterally. The great apes do it with no clothes at all. It's about the way you walk rather than what you wear. It's about the overall image you project.

But this doesn't mean you can get away with dressing inappropriately or badly—anyone can dress smartly. Borrow a decent outfit or buy a good suit cheaply. (No, no, don't buy full price and just put it on your credit card!) For the interview for my first casino job, I bought a fabulous jacket from a thrifty store— double breasted, wide satin lapels—and proper bow tie you had to tie yourself (none of those rubbish ones on elastic for me). I practiced for hours until I got it right and turned up for the first night looking more James Bond than trainee. I made a dramatic impression. Obviously, I had gotten it wrong and had to go and buy a simple black suit afterward, but I was remembered as somehow standing out, stylish, and not scruffy. And I got offered the trainee job despite not being in any way qualified for it. This stuff works, you know. Dress wealthy and people will assume you are and treat you accordingly. Learn style, class, and how the wealthy dress. Look poor, and you'll get poor service. And whatever you do, no bling. Yes, rich rap stars can get away with it, but you can't. Nor can I. Restrained elegance is what we shall aim for. Old money. Quality. Simple lines. Good haircut. Clean nails. You know the sort of stuff I mean.

Speculate to Accumulate (No, This Isn't Gambling)

We all know the actor who achieves overnight fame after one starring role, and everyone says how lucky he must have been. Luck? He starred in every school production. Studied at drama school for three years. Worked his socks off in some dreadful soap opera. Slaved on the stage for the entire summer theater run of *Our Town* by Thorton Wilder. Played an extra in HBO's *Extras*. Helped with *The Nutcracker* every Christmas—playing a sugarplum, of course. Finally landed his breakout job, his starring role, in some deservedly successful film. And everyone says, "How lucky you are!"

Getting wealthy is a bit like that. You toil away for years, and suddenly you are lucky. You scrimp and save and sacrifice, and gosh, how wonderful to be touched by fate's fickle finger!

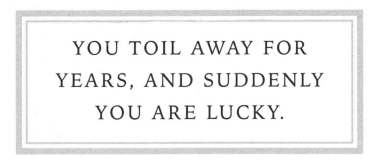

> ## YOU TOIL AWAY FOR YEARS, AND SUDDENLY YOU ARE LUCKY.

Well, the truth is that you have to speculate to accumulate. You have to be in it to win it. If you don't bet, you don't get. No, no, no. I am not suggesting gambling in any sense. If you invest on the stock exchange, after wisely taking advice and studying the companies and their performance, this is the safest form of gambling. If you stake it all on red, this is high-risk gambling. If you work your socks off for 20 years and finally it pays off, this is not gambling.

Speculate has, in fact, four meanings—to discuss, to think deeply, to invest, and to believe in something not entirely certain. I think that about sums up our pathway to prosperity.

- **Discuss**—Talk to everyone about wealth, and see what others think and do. Study them closely.
- **Think deeply**—Understand your subject.
- **Invest**—Speculate with your time and effort and life.
- **Believe in something not entirely certain**—There are no guarantees, but you should be able to shorten the odds considerably if you follow the rules others have forged for you.

I know you might have thought I want you to speculate with your hard-earned cash. I don't. I want you to speculate with your time and effort, forethought and planning, and energy and dedication. The more you put in, the more you'll get out.

On the other hand, you could go and blow it all on red. Only joking.

Decide Your Attitude toward Risk

Am I going to suggest that money can only be hard won by perilous investments and chancy ventures? No, I'm not. In that case, am I suggesting caution and that you should carefully hang onto every penny? No, I'm not advocating that either.

What I am suggesting is that it's entirely up to you what level of risk you feel happy with—it's no good for me to tell you what that level should be. You have to decide your own attitude toward and appetite for risk. Personally, I love the *idea* of sailing close to the wind financially. However, my attitude is definitely verging on the cautious side, so I don't take the risk. I find the risky schemes where you could blow it all or make a fortune hold some appeal, but I don't indulge my whims. I have young children, and they come first.

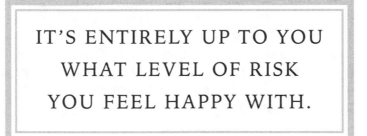

IT'S ENTIRELY UP TO YOU
WHAT LEVEL OF RISK
YOU FEEL HAPPY WITH.

After you decide your attitude toward risk, it makes your planning easier. It allows you to tailor how you intend to become prosperous. Hare or tortoise, I guess.

Obviously, your attitude will vary depending on the project. Things to take into consideration are

- **Your age**—We cope better with risk the younger we are.
- **Family commitments**—If, like me, you have young children, it does make you more cautious. If they've all left home, you might be prepared to push it a bit further.
- **Income and/or assets**—You need to work out the percentage of your wealth you are prepared to risk. The more you've got, the smaller the risk might be—unless you are prepared to lose the ranch, of course.

If you are going to take risks, then do try to offset them. Take out insurance if you like:

- Don't put all your eggs in one basket (more about this later).
- Consider how much stress and excitement you can handle.
- Look at the timing—long term against quick returns.
- Think about how much you can afford to risk—worst-case scenario stuff.
- How much information do you have? Too little increases risk.

The other thing to ponder is how you respond to the risks of life. Life in itself is risky, and nothing is certain. How do you cope when things go wrong? Are you positive, dynamic, enthusiastic, and up? Or do you get all gloomy and depressed and feel the glass is half empty? Know yourself, and know how you cope and how you respond to changes. And remember that risk doesn't mean bad. It means you don't know how it will all turn out.

If You Don't Trust Someone, Don't Do Business with Him

It's such a simple rule: We don't do business with people we don't trust. What more is there to say? Apart from that, this also includes companies, corporations, governments, you name it. And why don't we trust them? Because there is something adrift, something that rings that little warning bell inside us. There may be clear visible signs, but as often as not, there won't be. Mostly, this rule is about using your intuition, listening to your inner voice.

If you feel something, anything, is wrong, walk away. Listen to what is being said to you. There are unconscious clues your subconscious is picking up. If you ignore them, you'll invariably regret it. I've done it. We've all done it. I nearly did it again the other day. I nearly bought a car from an unreliable dealer. I knew he was unreliable, but I wanted the car. I knew the car would be unreliable. What is it that makes us overwrite all the warning signs? I did the only sensible thing—I phoned a friend. And he talked me out of it. Good man.

You can extend this rule to cover loads of situations, such as "If you don't trust your boss, don't work for him." "If you don't trust your babysitter, don't leave your kids with her." "If you don't feel comfortable with your financial adviser, get another."

Look, you can choose what you do and how you do it, but if you want to be a Rules Player, then you need to be assertive, stand up for what you know is right, and refuse to accept second best. Listen to your intuition. Be the biggest, boldest, and bravest. If the situation feels wrong, it probably is. If you don't get the right feelings about a person you are dealing with, find a way out.

If it waddles like a duck and quacks like a duck, chances are, it's a duck. Avoid it. Walk away. Hold on to your wallet and run.

> ## LISTEN TO YOUR INTUITION. BE THE BIGGEST, BOLDEST, AND BRAVEST.

It's Never Too Late to Start Getting Wealthy

It's very easy sometimes to believe that the hand we got dealt in life is all we have to play with. Or to say, "Ah well, I should have started a pension in my early twenties—it's too late now." But we can change anything we want—it's never too late to start being wealthy.

Look at Rule 1 again—anybody can make money. And it's not limited by your age or any other time factor. All it requires is that you shift your focus to becoming wealthy, and already things will happen without your having to do anything more. If you want more than the basics that the universe is going to give you, you will have to do more. But by shifting your focus, you will set wheels in motion, and prosperity will come to you. And no, this isn't mumbo jumbo. It's a universal fact. The fact that you do something—shift your focus—is enough.

No matter how long you have been going along a particular path—poverty, lack of success, whatever—it doesn't need much of a shift to alter your course. And altering your course can happen no matter how long you've left it. There is no such thing as too late. It's a bit like being an ocean liner. You may need a lot of space to stop, but it doesn't take much to get you to change direction. A couple of degrees on the wheel, and you'll be on a completely different course within a few miles.

In gaining prosperity, as in most things, there is a tipping point. After you've added on those couple of degrees to port or starboard, the resulting change in trajectory gets bigger and bigger in a sort of compound way.

It is also never too late to start investing in stocks, in shares, in a pension, in style, in quality, in yourself, in life. By staying alert and alive, we resist that decline into inactivity and apathy, which is such an aging attitude. My father-in-law (always such an inspiration) started another business when he was 75, and not just any old business either—it was in a new technology that most 50-year-olds were having trouble getting their head round.

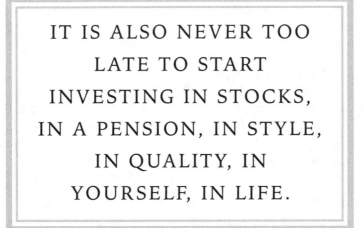

> IT IS ALSO NEVER TOO LATE TO START INVESTING IN STOCKS, IN A PENSION, IN STYLE, IN QUALITY, IN YOURSELF, IN LIFE.

However, if you think it is too late, it probably is. The secret is never to think that. If you think that you can give up easily, then you probably will. Don't think it. Look, we came into this book together to make money—some for you and some for me. I'm going to do my best, my damnedest, to help you increase your prosperity. If you think there are any barriers—age, sex, race, ability—then you are already on a losing path. Dump the preconceptions and trust me. It is never too late to begin. Start now.

Start Saving Young (or Teach Your Kids This One If It's Too Late for You)

Okay, it might be too late for you to start saving young. We can't go back. But you can certainly teach your kids the importance of learning this trick. And I'm not suggesting we scrimp and save to be able to save. Saving should be something you do naturally. I guess it's a trick you learn quickly if you are self-employed—or not, if you go bust. Every time you earn money, you put some aside for taxes. Failure to do so means scrambling around when the return is due and you have to find it. If you put aside more than you need, the leftovers become the savings. Obviously, you only fail to do this once or twice before it becomes a really easy thing to remember to do.

> ## IF YOU PUT ASIDE MORE THAN YOU NEED, THE LEFTOVERS BECOME THE SAVINGS.

I find that it is easier to have a "figure" so that you don't have to think too much. My own figure is 50 percent. Anything I earn, I put half straight into a savings account. I don't have to think about this. I know that some is for tax and the rest is for savings. Every now and again, I transfer the balance of what's left to a second savings account—a sort of super savings account. From the super savings account, I can transfer money to a pension fund, IRA, or whatever.

This, for me, is an easy way to save. I don't have to think too much about it. It is a method I pass on to my children—spend half your pocket money and save half. I hope they'll find this an easy method to pick up, a sort of savings muscle memory so that they will have a dollar or two when they need it at college or whatever.

I really wish I had (a) started saving young and (b) been taught to do so. Lots of really prosperous people have said that they had wealth management drummed into them from a very early age. It seems to be an essential part of prosperity gaining.

I am fascinated to watch my own children learning about money. There does seem to be a genetic predisposition for spending or saving. We treat all of them identically when it comes to money, but one child finds it easy to save; another is a fanatic spender and couldn't save anything to save himself; and one is oblivious to money either way.

I'm a great believer in making changes to correct basic flaws in one's upbringing. It's no good sitting around blaming others; you have to change it. I have to take responsibility and train myself. Obviously, this doesn't apply to being tidy.

Understand That Your Financial Needs Change at Different Stages of Your Life

Some cultures allow for a different focus, a different strategy, during different stages of life. For instance, up to 20 might be for being young and foolish and getting an education. Age 20 to 35 could be for getting married and raising a family. Age 35 to 55 might be for running your business and making your fortune. Life after that is for spiritual contemplation and retirement from the commercial world.

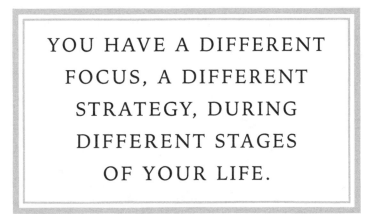

YOU HAVE A DIFFERENT FOCUS, A DIFFERENT STRATEGY, DURING DIFFERENT STAGES OF YOUR LIFE.

Essentially, your financial needs change over time, reflecting what is going on in your life at any stage, and the choices you make in your lifestyle at that time. You might need more money when raising a family, but maybe this is a time when you can usually cope better with a little adversity.

By the time your kids are in college, you definitely need loads more cash, or the poor darlings won't have enough to squander in the student union bar in the evenings, every evening. And when you hit retirement, you can downsize again—unless you intend to spend it all on expensive world cruises.

This rule is about checking where you are and what you need. And about knowing that the conditions that influence your needs do and will change. You have to make allowances for differing circumstances.

A bit of forward planning with this in mind will stand you in good stead. For example, if you're about to invest all your spare cash in a long-term investment scheme, remember that if you suddenly need a bit more money because you've taken maternity leave or you want to go on a world trip in a career break, your money will be tied up. Think it through, and anticipate possible future needs and changes.

So, quick exercise. Where are you in your life? How much do you need? What is the next stage for you? How much are you going to need?

You Have to Work Hard to Get Rich Enough Not to Have to Work Hard

I cannot emphasise how strongly I feel about this one. I watch and learn from the seriously wealthy and have reached the conclusion that in nearly every case, they worked like crazy to get where they are. They often started early. They worked late into the night. They sacrificed a lot. They didn't take long lunch breaks. They didn't waste time. They didn't watch television in the evenings. They worked their socks off. They knew money doesn't grow on trees.

> ## THEY DIDN'T WATCH TELEVISION IN THE EVENINGS. THEY WORKED THEIR SOCKS OFF.

If you, too, are serious about getting rich, then you, too, must do as they do. You are going to have to put in the hard work to get rich enough so that you don't have to work hard. But you must do the work first.

So, how dedicated are you? How serious are you? This is the point where we sort the wheat from the chaff, the men from the boys, the girls from the women, the runners-up from the winners.

RULE 29

Still here? Good. You are obviously committed. If you are prepared to put in the long hours and you put them in on the right things, you should succeed. Maybe not immediately. Maybe not with your first idea. But by slogging away, you will get there. How do I know this? Because I have done it. I'm not preaching from the wilderness. (I hope I'm not preaching at all.) I started out poor and worked long and hard and chose where to put my efforts carefully. And now I'm rich. It really is that simple. On the surface, it looks like luck. But that's because I make it look so. In *The Rules of Work*, I wrote about looking cool, looking laid back, looking effortless. I practice that a lot. I often go back to work very late at night after everyone else has gone to bed—or get up very early in the morning. Don't tell anyone, because I like the indolent image where everyone assumes I am a work-shy, lotus-eating, decadent loafer. But the reality is that I grind away. You have to.

I'll let you into the secret of the wealthy club—you need to work like you've never worked before. Work like there is no one watching. Work like you don't have a boss. Work like your life depends on it. The second secret is, you have to enjoy it. If it's a chore, you won't do it.

Let me make one very important point here. This Rule does NOT mean that if you work hard at *anything*, you will become wealthy. An office cleaner on minimum wage will not become rich by working all hours as an office cleaner or by cleaning really hard and thoroughly. He might, however, become rich by starting his own cleaning company, working very hard at getting it off the ground and finding new clients, and making sure his staff is great, happy, and motivated.

What I'm saying here is that even if you've got a great business idea or have some money to invest in shares, you will only maximize your return if you work really hard at your idea or invest the money wisely and manage it carefully. You have to put the effort in before you can reap the dividends.

Learn the Art of Deal Making

Deals are great. They make you money. Simple deal-making skills will serve you time and time again. You need to learn to be bold, to ask for more, to trade what you have for what you want.

Here is an example of successful deal making in action. Kyle MacDonald from Montreal, Canada, traded his way from one red paperclip to a house in the space of nine months. You can read more at http://oneredpaperclip.blogspot.com/, but essentially this is how he did it:

- He launched his Web site offering to swap his one red paper clip for anything.
- He swapped it for a green pen in the shape of a fish.
- He swapped this for a smiley face doorknob.
- He swapped this for a portable barbeque.
- He swapped this for a portable generator.
- He swapped this for an instant party pack and keg of beer.
- He swapped this for a snowmobile.
- He swapped this for a trip to British Columbia.
- He swapped this for a truck.
- He swapped this for a recording contract.
- And finally, he swapped this for a house in Phoenix, Colorado— admittedly only a year's lease, but hey … .

Eleven steps. Eleven little deals. Not bad. He says he is going to keep going until he owns a house. That's deal making.

So, lessons to be learned from Kyle:

- Never say you haven't got anything to start with.
- Always be open to opportunities.
- Be adaptable and flexible.
- Have a goal.
- Work diligently.
- Network like mad.
- Take advantage of free publicity.

In my business, I prefer to talk about "mutually profitable partnerships." These deals, where both parties benefit, are the best deals of all. Everybody feels happy with the outcome.

> # WHAT DO YOU
> # HAVE THAT OTHERS
> # MIGHT WANT?

What do you have that others might want? Think broadly here—not just possessions like Kyle, but also your skills and your knowledge. Your time and your ability and efforts. Who might want these, and what might you be able to ask for in return?

Learn the Art of Negotiating

If you are going to deal and trade and swap, you have to learn the art of negotiating. Basically, the art revolves around making the other person feel they are getting as much as you are.

I like to talk about partnerships. This is my way of making this happen. I'm genuinely not out to ruin anyone else's plans of getting rich. I don't need someone to fail to make me succeed. I figure we can all go forward together, and no one has to lose out. If I want someone to buy something from me, I expect them to make a profit on it and do well with it. I don't want to sell and run. I want repeat business. I want a decent reputation. I want to feel good about what I do. I want a partnership.

> I DON'T WANT TO SELL AND RUN. I WANT REPEAT BUSINESS. I WANT A DECENT REPUTATION.

RULE 31

The art of negotiating will stand you in good stead in so many different situations—from negotiating a simple pay rise to negotiating in your relationship with your partner to negotiating with your kids over pocket money. If you learn this art, everything will move along easily and smoothly, and you will get what you want—and they will get what they want, too. Win/win.

There are a number of rules about negotiating that you need to keep in mind:

- Always know your bottom line—the point beyond which you will not go.
- Always know what it is you want—the goal, the end product, the target. There's no use negotiating if you don't know what you are negotiating for.
- Always aim for win/win.
- Always remember that negotiating isn't just about stuff—it has powerful emotional ramifications as well.
- Know the importance of each point—some you can let go of, some you can't.
- Always be prepared to give up things to secure other things—be flexible and fluid.
- Always know as much as possible before you start—knowledge is power in these situations.
- Understand what people aren't saying as much as what they are saying—watch their body language and facial expressions.
- Stay cool and patient.
- Negotiate successfully for everything you want at the beginning—you can't negotiate afterward. No one will go back over a contract you've signed when you realize you don't like it.
- Find out exactly what others want (what they'll trade or concede), and get all their shopping list before you start negotiating. Hide yours.

- Don't make concessions—trade them.
- Create more variables—discounts, delivery, payments, stages, and so on.
- Go for the best deal you can possibly justify. Coming down later is easy; going up later is almost impossible.

I am always stunned and horrified by how often people go into situations—anything from a job to a relationship—without first finding out what they are embarking on, what is expected of them, what they are going to get out of it, what they expect their partner (boss, business buddy, lover, offspring, whoever) to get out of it, and where they expect to end up. You've got to discuss these things—and that really is the basic art: discussion. Bring things out into the open so that there are no assumptions. Assumptions are bad.

Small Economies Won't Make You Wealthy, but They Will Make You Miserable

Is it penny-wise and pound-foolish? I don't think so. I think that trying to make small economies to become prosperous is doomed to failure. It won't make you rich, but it will make you miserable. And being miserable isn't a good place to start out each day. You need a decent breakfast and a positive attitude. Cutting out your daily cappuccino might help you lose weight, and it might reduce your caffeine intake, but it isn't going to make you rich, and it might well make you feel miserable.

> ## CUTTING OUT YOUR DAILY CAPPUCCINO ISN'T GOING TO MAKE YOU RICH.

So, what about all that penny-pinching stuff? It seems to have been invented by the puritans—if you enjoy it, it has to be wrong. Some people get satisfaction out of being frugal, but if that isn't you, then don't deny yourself small pleasures in the belief that that's the way to wealth.

Hang on, though. Didn't I say in an earlier Rule that the rich are eagle-eyed and that you had to stop money leaks? Indeed. But that's different. While getting your finances in order is a good thing, going without isn't. Make sure you aren't giving money away by being careless (those are the leaks), but don't deny yourself the very small pleasures that enrich your life—just don't go crazy. If you can't afford what you want, buy less, but buy quality. Save up by all means for those big purchases or ask if you really need them, but don't start thinking that giving up little luxuries, little treats, little life enhancers, will somehow increase your wealth. It won't. It will keep you trapped in the poverty cycle. Escaping from the poverty cycle and the penury mindset is your key to success, your path to prosperity.

Wealthy people don't scrimp and save. Sure, some of them are quite tight-fisted, and you'd have to crowbar their wallets off them. But while they watch their money carefully, they don't cut out the odd cup of coffee or buy cheap condiments in the hope it will make them more wealthy. It obviously won't.

Like being on a diet, if you deny yourself every small pleasure, you'll probably fail. Little indulgences are the way forward. Now, who else is going to tell you that?

Understand That Working for Others Won't Necessarily Make You Rich—But It Might

Most of us assume that we'll never make it to greater prosperity while we are working for someone else—that only by being entrepreneurial will we become wealthy. And for a lot of us this may well be true—there is a limit as to how much you can earn per hour in return for your labor. However, there are some who do make it good this way.

We shouldn't overlook the fact that being employed may be the best route for us and that we don't have to run our own business. There are whole categories of employees who are doing quite nicely, thank you—for example, a friend of mine works in corporate insurance, and he's extremely wealthy thanks to large commission payments. He says he wouldn't be any better off working for himself.

Many people working in the computer business opted to become contractors because they assumed they would earn a lot more. Some did, but at the cost of stability. When the contracts dried up, some were worse off than when they were employed. But for some, this was indeed the best way to go, and they have made handsome sums by becoming self-employed.

I guess you have to keep an open mind about this one and not be driven by assumptions. You can make yourself quite unhappy by forcing yourself into self-employment if this isn't the right way for you. Perhaps the stability of employment is a greater priority, and you should stick with it and not feel compelled to start your own business.

RULE 33

> ## PERHAPS THE STABILITY OF EMPLOYMENT IS A GREATER PRIORITY AND YOU SHOULD STICK WITH IT.

The converse is true as well: understand that working for yourself might make you rich, but it might not. Nearly two-thirds of business startups end in failure within three years. Look around you, and you will see many examples of the small business owner struggling desperately. There's no certainty there. Working for yourself generally has higher earning potential, but not in every case. You have to look into it very closely—right business, right demand for your services, right time, enough effort, and so on.

There isn't the space or time here to go into all the pros and cons of working for yourself. Except to say it's one hell of a lot easier and much more fun working hard for yourself than for someone else. But what we are aiming for isn't freedom from employment but prosperity. Hence we have to be open to whichever means will hasten our achievement of that goal. Employment or going it alone? It entirely depends on which one will get us rich easiest, fastest, slickest. And your day job doesn't have to be your route to wealth at all.

The secret is not to close your mind to any opportunity to get rich. And staying employed doesn't mean not having a little eBay business on the side or a rental property to create a new income stream.

Don't Waste Time Procrastinating—Make Money Decisions Quickly

If you are out at sea and it becomes rough, you make for a safe harbor. Any port in a storm. You don't spend time procrastinating over whether the harbor has shower facilities or a branch of your favorite restaurant chain or cheaper moorings. No, you just get the hell out of the storm, while there's still space in the harbor, and be grateful it provides the one thing you really need—safety.

Making money is a bit like that. Sometimes, you just need to act. If you get some return on your action, it's better than doing nothing. This isn't complicated, but you'd be amazed how many people overlook this and think, "I'll decide how to invest that little lump sum I've saved up later—I can't decide whether to buy shares or put it in a savings account." So they do nothing, and the money sits in a current account earning no interest or, worse still, gets frittered away by default and inflation.

You don't have to think too deeply about this stuff. You don't have to think too hard. You don't even have to really think at all.

The samurai lived by a simple creed—no hesitation, no doubt, no surprise, no fear. It is simply the most brilliant strategy for doing anything. It basically says that when you decide on a course of action (or battle or combat), then be committed; know everything you need to know about it, don't be afraid, and get on with it as quickly as possible. If you've ever seen a samurai sword fight, you'll notice they circle each other, and then there is a dramatic burst of activity, a flurry of intense violence, and it's all over. One or the other or frequently both opponents are dead. The circling is not preparation—that was done over years and years of training. The circling is checking out your opponent—getting a feel for his mind. When samurai go into attack, it is a direct, swift, no hesitation attack. And your financial plans must have the same razor-sharp incisiveness about them.

> # THE SAMURAI LIVED BY A SIMPLE CREED—NO HESITATION, NO DOUBT, NO SURPRISE, NO FEAR.

Doing something is invariably better than doing nothing. And sometimes acting fast can be a lot better than holding out on a possibility. Suppose you buy and sell antiques and collectables as a money-making hobby. You might buy a plate for $20 and think you can sell it for $60, but somebody offers you $40 within an hour, and then you take the $40 and go and buy two more plates at $20 to sell in the same way. In some industries, it's called "churn"—keep things moving. Quickly weigh up the odds, consider the pros and cons, and then get on with it.

Work as if You Didn't Need the Money

Most of us work because we *do* need the money. But some of us let it show and some of us don't. If somebody looks as though he doesn't need the money, it's for one of two reasons. Either (a) he puts on a good act or (b) he genuinely enjoys his work and does it because he loves it—he would do it even if he didn't need the money.

Clearly (b) is a fantastic place to be and one we should all strive to get to. But even if that's not the case for you yet, there's a very good reason to act as if you would work irrespective of the financial return. If people think (or indeed know) that you need the money, it gives them power over you, and that puts you in a vulnerable position; it makes you insecure. If you work as if you don't need the money, they have no power. You have it instead.

> IF PEOPLE THINK THAT YOU NEED THE MONEY, IT GIVES THEM POWER OVER YOU, AND THAT MAKES YOU INSECURE.

RULE 35

Many years ago, I worked in a job I hated, and I was unhappy. Later on, I started a business that my heart wasn't really in, and it failed. But I have always written. Am I a writer? Not really. I don't write highbrow fiction. I wish I could, but I know my limitations and stick to writing about what I see other people doing. But writing is something I have always done—whether I get paid for it or not. Whether it gets published or not. And that's my secret; I do it because I passionately care about it. It is my heart and soul and belief and drive and ambition. It is so much a part of me that no one can touch it or have power over it or take it away. Do you know how happy that makes me? Do you know how rich that is making me?[11] Do you know how much power that gives me?

So, what's your secret? What makes your heart turn cartwheels? Where does your dream lie? You've got to be driven. Being prosperous has no room for "I don't know" or "I'm not sure." You've got to know; you've got to be sure. Why? Because that is what wealthy people do. They know where they are going and what they are going to do when they get there. They have passion, drive, ambition, and determination. They work because they want to.

Ah, but I hear you say, the passion and determination is something they are born with; it's in their personality. Perhaps it is. But it's also something you can emulate, copy, and mirror. Do like them to become like them. Work as if you didn't need the money. Aim for the point where you don't do anything unless your heart is in it.[12]

---

[11] And for once I don't mean financially happy, although that, too, is part of it in a big way.

[12] Obviously, even if you are following your dream, there will be moments, days, when you've had enough and you're sick of everything ... We're talking about what you overall enjoy, on the whole find pleasurable, and mostly glory in.

Spend Less Than You Earn

I'm amazed how many people flout this simple but most golden of all golden rules. You have to live within your means. Control your spending. Allow yourself to create a little bit of savings, with which to generate more income. (Remember the rabbit farm? You can't breed more rabbits if you sell them all.)

This Rule doesn't contradict Rule 32 about small economies not making you rich, by the way. You should live within your means but live well enough to be happy. If you don't earn enough to have champagne every week, then have it only once a month. But do have it if it makes you happy.

This is about being informed and in control. You need to know what your income is and what your expenses are. We'll talk later about how to curb spending and make savings and how to cut up your credit cards if they've let you down—they do that some-times, evil little things.

You also need to know

- Any expenditure that is likely to come up
- Any provision you've made for contingency plans
- Any future income you may be entitled to in the way of interest or investments coming to fruition

And that really is about it. Where people go wrong is *not* whether they earn enough or spend too much—both of those are fairly easy to overcome. No, the biggest mistake is not knowing what you are doing, where you are financially, and what is up ahead.

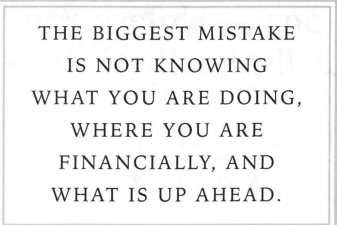

THE BIGGEST MISTAKE
IS NOT KNOWING
WHAT YOU ARE DOING,
WHERE YOU ARE
FINANCIALLY, AND
WHAT IS UP AHEAD.

I know it can be tough to live within your means, but if you are constantly in debt, all the prosperity that is rightfully yours is going to some faceless bank. I bet they're enjoying spending it. I bet they're having champagne more than once a week. Why encourage them?

I want you to know to the very week, the very hour, what you earn. And I want you to monitor what you spend, what it costs you to live—where you waste money, where you save money, and where you spend money wisely. As long as more is coming in than is going out, you're getting the basics right. If more is going out than is coming in, you need to take swift and effective action to address the situation.

Don't Borrow Money—Unless You Really, Really Have To

It's so important that I will repeat it: don't borrow money unless you really, really have to. And even then, don't. Not unless you are borrowing from someone who is lending it interest free, no strings, not secured against your house, and no potential for messing up friendships—and that sounds like la la land. Ha! There is no such thing as free money (or a free lunch).[13]

If someone lends it, he'll want it back—plus. And that plus is what kills most of us, stops us from becoming prosperous. It has to be nipped in the bud. And if it's too late for that, then it needs to be severely pruned. We have to get rid of that plus.

> ## IF SOMEONE LENDS MONEY, HE'LL WANT IT BACK—PLUS.

The plus is usually financial (i.e., interest on the loan), and this is what usually cripples people. However, the plus can be emotional also—if you borrow from friends and family, it can cause all kinds of other complications—it's never simple.

Pay off your loans and debts before you do anything else. It's the only way to get rid of the plus. I know, I know, lots of people borrow money to start their own business and then go on to

---

[13] There is such a thing, actually—check out http://myweb.tiscali.co.uk/freelunch/.

make millions, and what am I talking about—we all have to borrow, don't we? Do we? I have a friend who started his own business with three friends. They all put in $1,000 and ran the business for 15 years. Then they sold it for $86 million. Yep, and not a penny borrowed. The upshot was they had to share with no one—and at times like this, you don't want to share, no matter what your parents said about how we all should learn to share.

I have another friend who borrowed heavily to launch his business, which he successfully sold for $16 million. But nearly every penny of that went into loan repayments and interest. He was left with very little and, having not learned his lesson, proceeded to start another business with capital raised by loans. But he says he has learned a lot because this time he's only borrowed $6 million. Ho ho.

When you are starting a business, advisers often say it's okay to borrow from people you know because they are willing to support you, and so on. But the novelist Jilly Cooper says she is wary of lending money to friends because it is terribly difficult to see someone at Christmas and give them a hug knowing that person owes you $10,000. Personally, I would find it hard to hug someone who owed me a lot less than that!

Try not to borrow from

- Your parents
- Your children
- Other people's children
- Friends
- Lovers
- Passing strangers
- Loan sharks
- Banks
- Credit card companies
- Offshore investment bankers of any sort
- Me

Consider Consolidating Debts

Obviously, the best advice is not to get into debt in the first place. If it's a bit late for that nugget of wisdom, then you need to pay as little interest as you can while you are paying off your debts (which clearly you will be doing as quickly as possible). Consolidating debts is one way of doing this that might be right for you. What I am talking about here is stopping using three or four credit cards plus an overdraft plus a bank loan plus other borrowings. It is possible to consolidate all of them into one loan, tear up the cards (as if—you need industrial strength scissors, and here speaks a man who has cut up many a credit card), and pay off the overdraft. And, yes, I do understand the ease and usefulness of a credit card, but don't forget that good old stand-by—cash.

> ## DON'T FORGET THAT GOOD OLD STAND-BY—CASH.

A word of warning, however, if you do consolidate your debts, make sure you aren't turning short-term debts into long-term debts. The idea is strictly to pay off debt quickly.

If you do decide to consolidate your debts, here are some useful tips:

- I have a friend who wrote to all his creditors and offered them an immediate payment of 50 percent if they would write the debt off—this included all his credit card people. Surprisingly, every single one of them said yes, and he took out a bank loan and paid them all off without having to declare himself bankrupt. He thus consolidated his debts and reduced them by half. Brilliant.

- Never respond to any advertisements from companies offering to consolidate your debts for you—those ads are for people with more money than sense.

- Shop around for any pay-off loans—don't accept your bank's just because it is your bank—they may not be the cheapest by a long way.

- Don't secure anything against your home under any circumstances. If you do, you could lose your home if you don't keep up repayments. Is anything worth this risk? I don't think so.

- Check the small print regarding early settlements, and be sure you aren't going to be penalized if you settle early.

- Only take out one loan to consolidate, and only do this once—learn your lesson and move on.

- Pay off as quickly as you can afford—the longer the term, the more you'll have to pay in interest.

- If you must borrow, borrow against an asset you can resell (machine tool, delivery van) and try not to borrow more than the resale value.

- Buying on credit is a bit different. When Jack Cohen started Tesco, he negotiated the rent for his shop to be paid 3 months in arrear, he paid for his stock 3 months in arrear, and started taking money over the counter on day 1. By day 90 he had taken in a lot more than he owed.

Cultivate a Skill and It'll Repay You over and over Again

There's a saying that he who pays the piper calls the tune. And that's true. But the piper can decide how much he will charge for playing that tune if what he plays is

- In demand
- Rare
- Particularly difficult (or in some way unique) to play

Get yourself a decent instrument, a decent set of tunes, an unusual or quirky PR approach, and a unique spelling proposition. Create a name for yourself, and the world will beat a path to your door, and pay you handsomely.

When you can do something no one else can do—or as few people as is possible—you can pretty well name your price. And believe me, it doesn't have to be a particularly difficult skill, just one that somebody else wants and will pay for. Remember the guy who polishes the very best cars at a premium price? (*See Rule 7.*)

You could train to be a brain surgeon,[14] but that takes over ten years and aptitude and dedication and steady hands. So putting that aside, think about what you've got to offer. What are your skills, your talents, your strengths and weaknesses? Who needs those skills? How could you put them to best use? How do you tell the people who need these skills that you have them? What skill can you master to meet a need that's out there waiting to be met?

---

[14] Neurosurgeon as they are properly titled.

> ## WHEN YOU CAN DO SOMETHING NO ONE ELSE CAN DO—OR AS FEW PEOPLE AS IS POSSIBLE—YOU CAN PRETTY WELL NAME YOUR PRICE.

For this exercise, you are not allowed to say

- Don't know
- Not sure
- Nothing really
- Not a lot
- What do you mean? Talent? Skills? Me?

Come on, we all have something we can do or could do that is special to us, that we feel we could make a fortune from if only someone would give us a break.[15] We all have a dream we could follow, a plan we dare carry out. Perhaps all we need is a shove, a push in the right direction, a wake-up call to get up off our backside and actually do something. Well, this is it. WAKE UP. GET ON WITH IT.

---

[15] No one gives you a break—you create breaks, you go out there and wrestle breaks to the ground and beat them into submission, you lure them out of their caves with sweets on a stick, you track them down and hunt them with an opportunity gun, you stay in their face until they give in—but no one gives them away.

Pay Off Your Loans and Debts as a Priority

Do you clear your credit card balance every month? If you do, and you don't have any other outstanding loans/debts, then well done, you. You're not wasting money paying interest, and you're already in a strong position to go forward. Skip the rest of this Rule and carry on.

If you *do* have a credit card balance (or five), an overdraft, or other loans or debts[16], then you certainly aren't alone. It's so easy to get credit these days, and we live in a "have it now, pay later" society. Trouble is, debt bogs us down and holds us back. We're simply throwing money away paying off the interest. (You borrow, say, $20,000, and you can end up paying several thousand extra dollars back in interest. The actual amount you end up paying depends on how long you borrow for, as well as the interest rate you're being charged.) Debt is a millstone around the neck—it makes you feel bad, it's always there nagging away at the back of your mind, and it can easily become a major problem that affects your health as well as your wealth.

> ## DEBT BOGS US DOWN AND HOLDS US BACK.

---

[16] We don't include mortgages in this category, by the way. Although strictly speaking, a mortgage is a loan, it's also an investment (we hope) and, therefore, is a special case.

There's no doubt about it. The very first thing you need to do on your wealth quest is to get loans/debts paid off as soon as possible and do nothing else until that's done. There's no point at all starting to put money into a savings account, earning say 5 percent interest, if you are at the same time paying 10 percent interest on money you owe to the bank or somebody else. It doesn't make sense. The simple truth is that those who borrow almost always pay a higher rate of interest than the rate received by those who save.

I acknowledge that you may, in fact, have found a special situation where you can borrow money at a very low rate of interest and believe you can invest that money for a bigger return, but I say be very, very, very careful indeed. You are playing with fire here, and unless the investment is absolutely risk free (which I doubt), pay the debt/loan off as fast as you possibly can.

I should stress here that there are a few possible special exemptions to this Rule, such as if you've borrowed to invest in a business and you really know what you're doing. We're actually talking mainly about personal debt in this Rule.

I'm not playing down how difficult it is to become debt free, but it has to be done. Make a plan as to how you're going to get rid of your debt. Start by paying off the highest interest debt first if you've more than one. Motivation is vital, as this is short-term pain for long-term gain.

And, of course, when you finally make it to debt free, you're never going there again, are you? (*See Rule 36.*) Of course, you aren't. You're a Rules Player now.

Don't Be Too Busy Earning a Living to Make Some Money

It's easily done. You needed a job to survive like we all do. Then you got into working for a living, and it took up such a huge amount of your time and energies that there was none left over to spend thinking about what you could be doing differently, extra, or smarter, to make more money. How many of us are guilty of letting our financial affairs slide because, quite frankly, we feel there are better things to do with our precious free time than come to terms with our finances or plan a long overdue life/career change?

Sometimes, we're so busy doing our jobs, we forget the end goal—making some real money. Well, to become wealthy, you absolutely have to remember to lift your head above your 9 to 5 (or 8 to 8, or whatever hours you work) and give yourself a chance to think about the bigger picture—and take action.

Lots and lots of people work to live—and without them, the rich couldn't get richer. And this doesn't mean the workers are being exploited or used. It's just that if people choose to be drudges and invest all their time and energy in working for wages, there will always be other people who will be quick to see an opportunity and become prosperous, simply because they had their heads up and could see further.

If you do work for a living and don't confidently expect that job to make you rich, you must be doing it for love, right? No, this isn't a trick question. It is about prioritizing our ambitions. If we go to work solely for money, it makes sense to earn as much as we can, as we want.

> # IF WE GO TO WORK SOLELY FOR MONEY, IT MAKES SENSE TO EARN AS MUCH AS WE CAN.

If you love what you do, then if the money doesn't come with it, you need to create a strategy for wealth creation that doesn't rely on the "day job" income. It's great that you love what you do, but if you also want wealth, you need to make sure you aren't so busy doing it that you forget to work out how you're going to get wealthy doing it, or what other actions or strategies you need to create a second income or alternative revenue generator.

If you are unhappy with your pay or hate your job, then you have to question why you're still doing it and what else you could do. The worst possible scenario is that you don't feel fulfilled or rewarded in your job but you are so busy doing it that you don't have time to create a plan that will bring you greater prosperity and happiness. While you've got your head down earning a living, a million and one opportunities to become prosperous have just passed over your head, and you didn't see them. Imagine waking up in ten years' time and realizing that's what you'd done. If this is your situation, then do something now. Change your perspective and seize the day.

RULE 42

Save in Big Chunks— or Should You?

I always thought that if I could get my hands on a big chunk, I would put loads of it away, and that would be a brilliant way of saving. I have a friend who says that is nonsense and that the drip-by-drip effect is the best way to save. Who is right and who is wrong? Obviously, I must be right. It's my book, after all.

Let us consider it a bit more logically. Suppose I save a big chunk. Let's say I get $20,000 for some work I do or something I sell. I spend half and save half. And I do this when I am 50. How much do I have at retirement?

My friend saves a measly, miserly $10 a month—small potatoes, I say. But he did start early—at 20, and never missed a month. Who is going to retire big time, and who is going to be reusing tea bags? Come on, come on, you can work this stuff out in your head, can't you? No? Okay, look at the chart on the next page (assuming a modest 5 percent interest per annum).

See, I told you I was right ... but not by much. Hope you have learned a valuable lesson here. It's good to be prudent and save regularly but in the long run a big chunk saved later in life will bring home the bacon just as easily.

---

[17] I know, I know, he won't get 5 percent on the entire amount because he won't have the full $120 until the end of year 1, but this is just an example.

[18] I'm assuming I invest at the beginning of the year.

Year	My friend aged 20 at $10 per month	Me, who doesn't save a thing until I'm 50—ha!
1	$126[17]	
2	$258	
3	$397	
4	$543	
5	$696	
6	$857	
7	$1,025	
8	$1,202	
9	$1,398	
10	$1,594	
11	$1,800	
12	$2,016	
13	$2,243	
14	$2,421	
15	$2,668	
16	$2,927	
17	$3,199	
18	$3,485	
19	$4,163	
20	$4,497	
21	$4,847	
22	$5,215	
23	$5,601	
24	$6,007	
25	$6,433	
26	$6,880	
27	$7,350	
28	$7,843	
29	$8,361	
30	$8,905	This is the year I make my big savings killing with $10,000 + 5% = $10,500[18]
31	$9,476	$11,025
32	$10,075	$11,576
33	$10,704	$12,154
34	$11,365	$12,761
35	$12,059	$13,399
36	$12,787	$14,068
37	$13,552	$14,771
38	$14,355	$15,509
39	$15,198	$16,284
40	$16,083	$17,098
41	$17,013	$17,952
42	$17,989	$18,849
43	$19,014	$19,791
44	$20,090	$20,780
45	$21,220	$21,819
Totals	$21,220	$21,819

Don't Rent, Buy

We all need somewhere to live. We, therefore, have the choice as to whether to rent the roof over our head or buy it. Most of us can't afford to buy outright (I doubt you'd be reading this book if you were in this category), so to buy, we need to borrow a lump sum of money to buy with. But hang on. Haven't we said that borrowing is bad, bad, bad, and we shouldn't do it? Haven't we said that this way madness lies, because you pay so much interest on what you borrow and so on? Indeed we have.

So how can you own and not borrow, buy and not have a mortgage?

The answer is that a mortgage can actually be viewed as an investment rather than a borrowing. If you buy a property with a mortgage, you make a monthly investment. The fact you pay that to a mortgage company we can gloss over. You see, in the longer term (and if you're lucky, the shorter term, too), you can reasonably expect that the interest you pay on your mortgage

> ## SO HOW CAN YOU OWN AND NOT BORROW, BUY AND NOT HAVE A MORTGAGE?

will be less than the increase in the value of your property. What you are banking on is that the value of your home will, in the longer term, go up and, therefore, you have invested whatever deposit you put down and your mortgage money.

Renting, on the other hand, is not an investment. You will never see that money again. Of that there is no doubt.

With a mortgage, you stand a good chance in the long term of seeing your mortgage payments lead to an increase in the value of your house. When you sell, you get that increase in value.

There are those who believe that buying your home instead of renting brings with it huge stresses and means you have less fun. It's actually not the ownership that causes stress, it's how much you borrow to do it and what that means for your overall financial picture. The lesson is to think carefully about how much your mortgage repayments will be and that you are able and willing to pay them.

Of course, if you buy, there are no guarantees your home will increase in value—there will be house price slumps—but over time, chances are that they recover and go on to increase again. Ideally, buy cheap and sell for a lot more. You then have a choice: Invest the profits in the next property without borrowing any more, and in doing so, you decrease the mortgage each time. Eventually you own outright, and without mortgage payments, you have somewhere to live and don't have to pay for it at all any more.

Alternatively, you can do what most people do and buy a bigger, better, more expensive house. This isn't a wealth creation strategy, but it can be what you wanted your wealth for, which makes it fine by me.

RULE 44

Understand What Investing Really Means

Many investments have a twofold purpose: They generate income, and they increase in value. In other words, if you invest a lump sum (this is known as *capital*), you get regular small payments of some kind, *and* the actual value of the capital itself increases, i.e., the lump sum gets bigger.

Let's suppose you invest in property. In an ideal world, you should be able to rent it out, thus providing the regular small payments in the form of rental income, and the value of the property should go up also, so your capital increases in value over time.

Likewise, shares should pay out dividends (generate income) and should be worth more than you bought them for when you sell some time later (increase in value). You get the idea. And notice I say "should" rather than "will"—nothing is certain in this game.

You can, of course, invest in almost anything you want:

- Company shares
- Your brother's harebrained buy-an-old-boat-and-fix-it-up-and-sell-it-for-a-fortune scheme
- Fine wines, paintings, Krugerrands, classic cars, rare books, Georgian glass
- Pension funds and such, including savings and deposit accounts
- Inventions and new product development
- Ideas and people
- Theater shows, films, TV program development

And it doesn't have to be just plain old investment. There is also

- Sponsorship such as race cars, football teams, and so on to raise brand awareness (hopefully yours and not just the race car or football team).
- Angelic capital—you invest in people and ideas in an altruistic way rather than purely as a money-making venture (as opposed to venture capital, where you invest in people and ideas purely as a money-making venture).

Remember that investments of any sort are a form of gambling no matter which way you look at them. And you can lose. Ask Christie's if you don't believe me.

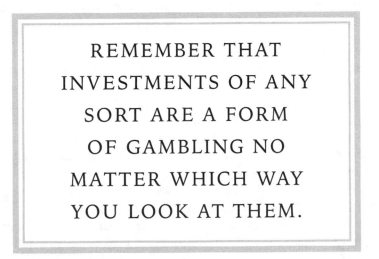

REMEMBER THAT
INVESTMENTS OF ANY
SORT ARE A FORM
OF GAMBLING NO
MATTER WHICH WAY
YOU LOOK AT THEM.

On the other hand, investing in a broad range of low-risk investments can still net returns worth having.

Build a Bit of Capital; Then Invest It Wisely

Lots of people dont't get prosperous because, as we saw earlier, they are too lazy. But a lot fail because they don't know what to do when they start to earn some money. It's easy to think, after you've got your hands on a bit, that you have earned it, you deserve it, you're gong to spend it. You *have* earned it—assuming you haven't robbed anyone to get it—and, yes, you probably *do* derserve it. But no, don't spend it all now, no matter how much you want that new car, holiday, cottage by the sea, whatever.

I've done it. I guess we all have. I once got a massive tax rebate. I don't remember why I was being taxed so highly, but I was for several years, and when they repaid me, it was quite a handsome sum. And, of course, I blew it, on a spendid holiday. But that's the difference between the rich and the not so well-off. The rich see a sudden windfall like that as an opportunity to make some more money out of it. The not so well-off remain not so well-off because they see it as an opportunity to have some fun. Nothing wrong with that if that's what you want in life—instant pleasure. But if you want greater wealth and pleasure (albeit delayed), then you must learn as I did that when you get your hands on a lump sum, or build some up, you must immediately put it to good use. And, frankly, the only good use is as a starter kit for prosperity.

And it isn't lost, merely put to one side to work for you. After it has grown and attracted lots more lovely money, you can have all the holidays you want. But you have to wait, and you have to use that starter kit well and wisely. Guides who make their living from tips find it wise to put something in the tip plate first. You have to put a coin or two in the plate or no one else will tip.

Street musicians do the same thing, put a coin or two into the hat to get the crowd going. No one will put anything into an empty hat. What you are going to do is load your prosperity hat.

> # NO ONE WILL PUT ANYTHING INTO AN EMPTY HAT.

Ah, but I hear you say, i'm never going to get my hands on a lump sum. Not true. You get your hands on a lump sum every week of your life in the form of wages—I'm assuming you do have a job. You choose what you spend that money on—mortgage, food, car, entertainment, and so on. But if you want a way out of that particular lifestyle and into another, you have to be proactive about it. And the way you start it is to put something aside each week to build up tht lump sum. When you have something built up, think about where that money is going to generate you more money, and get it invested. Ideally, you need to turn that money into an asset that will generate more revenue for you—be it a stock, a property you can rent out, or something else. Wealth happens slowly over a period of time when you turn surplus cash into something that will work for you.

Understand That Property, in the Long Run, Will Not Outpace Shares

So, you've built up a bit of money to invest—where to put it? Property and shares are two popular choices, but which to choose?

In the aftermath of the "dot-com" crash of 2000, when share prices started to plummet, many people turned from investing in shares to investing in property. It's not surprising, really. Many people who invested heavily in shares in the late 1990s saw the value of many of those shares drop so much it really hurt, and some companies folded completely, meaning investors lost all their money.

With people turning in huge numbers from shares to property, the rental real estate market boomed, and with greater demand from investor buyers, house prices rose. Eventually, the market reached a point where in some areas there was a glut of property available to rent, and income from rental properties failed to match expectations (supply outstripping demand). However, those early into the rental property boom who bought in the right areas did well. In the years since 2000, however, share prices have recovered, and those who could hold on to their shares on the whole have seen their value climb again.

So what's the right thing to do? Property or shares? Well, shorter-term blips notwithstanding, in the longer run, shares will outperform property.

Don't get me wrong—there's always a place for property. It's about getting yourself a good spread of investments—a portfolio as the professionals like to call it. Any decent investment portfolio is going to include property.

One big advantage of investing in property is that you can live in it. (As we said in Rule 43, you have to live somewhere and you can't live in cocoa futures.) Alternatively, if you're buying to lease, you will get income from the rental of the property (though you have to be extremely careful that the rent is as much as you hope it will be, that you are sure there is enough demand for rental properties in that area, and so on).

With shares, you hope to get regular income in the form of dividends paid to shareholders, but the greatest return usually comes from a long-term increase in share prices. Quite simply, as companies have greater potential for growth than property, the longer-term picture should see shares giving you a greater return. I stress potential here because it doesn't always get realized—the value of your shares, or your property, can go down as well as up. There's always risk. The other reason to prefer shares to property alone is that shares—especially a nice well-balanced portfolio— will give you a decent risk spread. The more variety, the less the risk. Did you know that in a slump, baked bean sales go up?

> ## ANY DECENT INVESTMENT PORTFOLIO IS GOING TO INCLUDE PROPERTY.

Master the Art of Selling

Just as deal-making is a vital skill, so is selling—and they aren't always the same thing. You sell stuff outside of deals. Indeed, one of the most important things you have to sell in life to increase your prosperity is yourself.

Selling is the bedrock upon which every fortune is built. Whatever you do to make yourself prosperous will involve selling: selling your skills, selling things, selling ideas. You can't make money without selling. Selling is where it's at. Every rich person knows this simple fact. Every poor person doesn't.

In an ideal world, you should aim to sell

- Yourself and your abilities, skills, and attributes (every minute of every day)
- Something while you're asleep
- In countries you've not only never been to but also have never heard of
- Via other people, so someone else is selling for you
- Things that are incredibly cheap to produce and give you a really healthy return
- Things other people make and finance for you
- Things that have a 99 percent penetration into every household
- Things that store, transport, and stack easily

The list is probably endless. But where people go wrong is when they try to sell things that no one really wants. Unless, of course, you are Ken Hakuta and you invent wacky wall, walker toys.

Now there's a market I never thought of.

Don't go thinking selling is for sales reps in shiny suits. Every time Richard Branson appears on television busy with a hot air balloon, he is selling—selling his entire brand. Clever man. Clever selling.

I like the young man Alex Tew who started college recently. He wanted to become a millionaire and realized that if he had a million things, he could sell them all for $1 and achieve his goal. And he realized a Web page has 1 million pixels. He then set about selling each one for $1 to advertisers. You need a block of around 400 (thus costing you $400) to be seen, but he sold half by Christmas and the rest within his first year at college. Head down? I don't think so. You can see the result at http://www.milliondollarhomepage.com/—and yes, I supported his venture and paid him $400 for advertising my business. I figured such an enterprising young man needed a monetary round of applause for ingenuity, cleverness, and innovation.

Don't Believe You Can Always Win

There is an entire list of things and people you can't beat, so it might be best to be cautious around them. They include the bookies (and anyone else trying to take money from you for gambling—casino owners, card sharps, race courses, online gambling Web sites, and so on), the tax authorities, speed cameras, the government, your mother, the police, your kids, and death.

Dan Brown, author of *The Da Vinci Code,* was sued by the authors of another book, *Holy Blood, Holy Grail,* because they believed he had plagiarized their work. They lost. They lost big time. They lost somewhere in the region of $3 million including costs.

They probably believed quite sincerely in the merits of their case. But did anybody tell them they were unlikely to win? It'd be fascinating to know whether anybody advised them not to proceed because they would probably lose.

The reason to be very cautious in your dealings with bookies, lawers, accountants, and such is that they have knowledge you don't. They are holders of secrets that can enable them (if they so choose) to make money out of you purely because of your ignorance.

And don't get all moralistic on me and try to change the system. These are facts of life. Live with them. Work them. You won't get rid of them. You can't beat the bookies—or the odds—so don't go trying or attempting to get rid of them on the grounds that they are making money out of the poor, innocent, gullible public. Trouble is, the poor, innocent, gullible public walk in there with their wallets open crying, "Help yourself." And then they complain they are broke, no one gives them a chance, life isn't fair, no one likes them, it's not their fault, there ought to be a law against it, and so on. Remember that there are sharks out there.

> REMEMBER THAT
> THERE ARE SHARKS
> OUT THERE.

RULE 49

Understand How the Stock Market *Really* Works

It's simple. People buy, sell, and trade investments—called stocks—that they have made in companies. So, how does it all work? And, more importantly, *what* works?

The easy answer to the last question is "Buy low; sell high," but don't you just know that there's more to it than that? The question of deciding what to buy, how much to pay for it, and when to buy (and then sell) it has been the subject of entire libraries of books, most of them bigger than this one, so I'll limit my contribution to a few choice rules. The first of these is to understand the real forces at play: *value* and *speculation*.

Personally, I think economists were put on this earth to make astrologers look good, but I'm not averse to quoting them. One of the most quotable, John Maynard Keynes, once said that the stock market is just like a beauty contest.

Now, when he said that, he didn't mean that stockbrokers should abandon their suits for swimwear and profess a desire for working with children or for world peace. He was referring to a type of British beauty contest that used to be run by London newspapers, in which readers could win a prize by picking the beauty whose photograph was deemed to be the most beautiful by the greatest number of other readers. This meant that winning was not about picking the prettiest, or even about predicting which the average reader would think the prettiest. But instead, winning became a game of anticipating what the average reader would expect the average choice to be. And this, believed Keynes, was how the stock market works. Investors try to make money by buying stocks that they think other investors will want to buy in the future, and the price that they're pre-pared to pay for a stock depends less on the fundamental value of the company than on their expectations of what everybody else will be willing to pay for it. That's the essence of speculation in the stock market, and that's why the fundamental value of a stock and its price on any given day can be so different.

Speculating on stock market movements is great fun if you want to observe mass psychology in action, but in an uncertain world, it's not the road to wealth. If you really want to accumulate wealth in the stock market, here's my rule: Get rich slowly, but surely, with value. Ignore all the noise, the clamour about what this piece of news or that piece of gossip means for a price. Stay away from the "proven" techniques for predicting what prices will do tomorrow based on what they did yesterday—technical analysis! Don't be fooled by the rational-sounding label, it's irra-tional—and resist, please resist, the temptation to dive in and out of stocks chasing a quick buck. If you're going to invest in shares, look for value. Look for companies whose price doesn't reflect their worth. Look for companies that make or do some-thing that people will find more valuable in the future, and look for companies whose value is appreciated by the investment funds. (We'll meet them in Rule 50.)

After youu find those stocks, buy them, and unless the funda-mentals change, buy them for the long run. Wait for their value to appreciate, and watch as your wealth accumulates.

So, to buy the right stocks at the right price, don't follow the crowd—find the value. That's easier said than done, you might say, and you'd be right. It can take a lot of research, but you can make it easier if you follow the next Rule.

RULE 50

Only Buy Shares (or Anything) You Can Understand

Another Rule to engrave on your heart: Buying shares—or anything else to sell to make money—is just another form of gambling. When I worked as a casino manager, it was well recognized that there was a hierarchy of casinos. At the bottom were the ones with the slot machines and noisy, brash atmosphere. At the top were the gentlemen's clubs where it was all smoked glass and diffused lighting. Gamblers, of course, recognised the hierarchy and felt that the latter were somehow "cleaner." Similarly, most people view the stock market as in some way more refined, sophisticated—and thus free of risk or odds or danger. But it is all gambling. Nothing is certain.

If you are going to gamble on shares (or anything else you want to buy and sell), then reduce the odds as much as possible and only invest in or buy things you know and understand. By doing this, you eliminate a lot of the mystique that can lead you to stake more than you intend, take risks you wouldn't normally, or be bamboozled by slick marketing spiel.

If you shop at Nordstrom, and you see that the new product ranges are good and that the stores are full and you hear people raving about how Nordstrom has improved this year, buy Nordstrom shares. If you keep studying the stores and listening to people shopping, you will quickly notice if it continues to be a good investment.

> # CUT THE ODDS DOWN AS LOW AS POSSIBLE, AND ONLY INVEST IN OR BUY THINGS YOU UNDERSTAND.

Just be careful you are aware if you are buying with your head or heart. I have a friend who only invests in green (environmentally concerned) companies. He moves about with an air of moral superiority. He believes he has bought a ticket to heaven by doing this. He is a gambler. He doesn't realize this. Is he buying with his head and his heart? If you find investments in something you love, be clear if you are buying as an investment on business principles or simply because you want to. If your rational market analysis says that wind farms are the future and will be a growing industry with big returns, then fantastic; you can invest with head and heart.

If you don't really understand a particular sector of business and don't intend to put the work in to get to know it well, you'll almost certainly be better off investing in something else. If you want to invest in shares but don't want to do all the homework and make all the decisions yourself, you can use an investment fund. And that brings us conveniently to our next Rule.

RULE 51

By All Means, Use the Investment Professionals (but Don't Be Used by Them)

As you've probably guessed from Rule 49, most of those who pick their own stocks like to think that they can see value where others can't. Of course, we don't like to look too often to see if our track record backs that up, and I'm sure many a Rules Player has made dumb investment decisions. If you don't trust yourself to make clever decisions every time, or perhaps simply want to save the occasional investment decision for yourself and let someone who knows more than you do take care of the rest, then it's okay to use the professionals.

When it comes to investment, the professionals cluster wherever you can find tall buildings and long lunches. Wall Street, Singapore, London...they're all positively teeming with investment experts ready to put their big brains and even bigger computers to work on your behalf. All for just a teensy-weensy fee, of course.

Well gold, as they say, may be bought too dear. I've often wondered just whose interests these professionals are serving. I certainly know a friend who's studied them and written about them, and who swears blind that there are crooks in the Stock Exchange, and that at least Dick Turpin "had the decency to wear a mask and not a pin-striped suit." Forgive me if you are a stockbroker—my friend may be just a touch paranoid—but personally, I believe that if you're going to use the pin-stripes to manage some of your stock-market investments, make sure you use them wisely. That's a big if, and that's what this rule's all about. How to use them to *make* more money, not *take* your money.

> # MOST OF THEM TRY HARD, THEY REALLY DO, BUT IN THE END, MOST OF THEM FAIL TO GROW MONEY ANY FASTER THAN THE MARKET. SO, DON'T PAY THEM FOR TRYING.

Now, pay attention to this bit—it's really, really important. First, they will tell you that they can take your money, invest it actively, and *beat* the market. That they *do* beat the market and that they *will* beat the market. They may even have some colorful charts to show you how they beat the market, *every* year. Apart from last year, of course. (And that was just a blip, a short-term correction you know, everybody took a bath on that one, but *next* year . . .) Just sign here, sit back, and you'll soon be worth more than Warren Buffett on a hot streak. Sounds too good to be true? Yep, it's wishful thinking and flawed logic in equal measures.

To put it simply, for somebody to be doing better than average, somebody else must be doing worse, and because the big firms invest most of the money in the market, who are they beating? Themselves? Right, and here's the ugly little truth about the investment industry. In any given year, some will come out ahead and some will lose, but over the long term, the market beats most of them, most of the time. Oh I'm sure many of them try hard, they really do, but in the end, nearly all of them fail to grow money any faster than the market. So, don't pay them for trying.

A sure-fire scheme for predicting winners? Unlikely. A hot tip for technology stocks? Hot air. Ask yourself this. If, like most people, you read the brochure, listen to the adviser (who's on a commission) and buy into a fund aiming to beat the market, what's the *one* thing that you can be sure will be higher than average? The returns? Or the fees? You know the answer to that one, don't you?

If you want help to put your money in the markets, without putting much of it in someone else's pockets, keep it simple.

If you don't have the time or know-how to carefully research the best active fund, follow the rule that *less is more* (and usually comes cheaper). Put your trust in funds that don't charge you big fees for taking big risks with a succession of clever strategies to beat the house. Pick ones managed by people who know enough to know that, in the long run, they won't beat the house by chasing higher returns from one stock to the next. Pick ones managed by people who'll invest your money, with minimum fuss and minimum fees, in a good range of stocks that replicate the market and then go to lunch. Then, you can sleep at night (or get back to reading this book) safe in the knowledge that your money is in the market, quietly working away on your behalf.

If you're wondering where to find these funds, they'll be called index funds or tracker funds. Of course, they pay less commission to middlemen and spend less money on advertising, and so their brochure may be the last one out of your financial adviser's briefcase, but when it comes to using investment professionals, start by putting your trust in time, not clever tactics. You can take a more active approach as your experience grows, but believe me, the fees will be smaller.

If You Are Going to Get Financial Advice, Pay for It

Boy, are there a lot of people out there waiting and wanting to give you financial help, advice, information, tips, and guidance. Great—learn early on to be very careful who you take advice from if you want to hang on to your wealth.

There are two groups of people to whom you may turn in the event of needing said advice, help, guidance, whatever. First, there are skilled professionals who carry indemnity insurance, so you can sue them—and expect to get a payout—in the unlikely event the information they give you is erroneous, wrong, or dangerously bad. If they stand by their advice, you should make sure provision is there so that you get paid if it is wrong. That keeps 'em on their toes. These people you pay and their fee entitles them to talk to you about your money.

Second, there are very rich people. Listen to them, unless they won their money on the lottery, inherited it, robbed a bank to get it, or bought a load of drugs in Marrakech and sold them in the local nightclub. (Actually, their entrepreneurial skills might be worth something even if their honesty or honor isn't.)

Those are the only two categories open to you. The ones closed to you include friends and family, well-meaning acquaintances (even if they do have a dollar or two of their own), TV programs, and the Internet.

You must make sure any financial advice comes from someone who carries a recognizable qualification or membership of a suitable organization—that includes the very, very rich club.

RULE 52

Make sure you know that they know what they are doing. The textile millionaire Joe Hyman used to say that in order of honesty, the three types of banks were (1) high-street banks (2) mountebanks and (3) merchant banks.

MAKE SURE ANY FINANCIAL ADVICE COMES FROM SOMEONE WHO CARRIES MEMBERSHIP OF A SUITABLE ORGANIZATION—THAT INCLUDES THE VERY, VERY RICH CLUB

There are two types of advisers in my experience: (a) those who stop you making an ass of yourself and (b) those who tell you you've made an ass of yourself after you've done it. You want category (a). You'll get loads and loads in category (b).

When it comes to professional financial advisers, there are another two categories: (a) those who deal with your finances and (b) those who try to sell you products. Avoid (b) like the plague.

RULE 52

Any financial adviser you use should be independent—i.e. he should not be restricted to providing advice from a limited range of products offered by the company he works for—it's the difference between buying a suit off the rack—a best fit—or buying something tailormade to fit your requirements precisely.

You should also insist on paying for the advice by means of an agreed fee—not by commission on the policies you take out or the products or investments they sell you. It's tempting to go down the commission route because it sounds like you get better value. (The financial adviser gets paid by the companies whose policies or investments he sells you.) It may sound like better value (great—somebody else pays the adviser for you!), but it may not be better advice. You want impartial advice that is exactly tailored to your circumstances, and paying for the advice is the only way to be sure you get it and you aren't sold a lot of policies or investments from companies that pay the best commission.

Don't Fiddle

When you've worked out a strategy, leave it alone. There is no point fiddling—you're unlikely to make it any better, and you might make it worse. Not only that, but you could incur lots of extra charges or penalties if you start changing things after a short time. You have to know when to leave things alone. It's like the proverb "look before you leap." Look long and hard. Then, make your plan and take your decisions. Then, leave it alone—don't mess with it.

Looking is weighing the odds, seeking advice, and considering the pros and cons. Leaping is acting on all that information. But after you have decided to leap, get on with it. When you have formulated your plan, your objective, your strategy, your goals and targets, and ambitions and destinations, be committed.

It is so easy to get scared or panicky. We all fear unemployment, poverty, financial traps, falling behind, falling below, falling in debt. I've been there. Having made a plan, I was paralyzed by fear into staying at a job for years because I didn't believe I could survive outside it. After I stepped outside, I survived just fine. We always do.

Plans and small fish require the same amount of cooking. After they're in the pan, leave them alone, or they'll fall apart. Don't keep stirring, or they'll disintegrate. Don't keep fiddling, tinkering, changing your mind, and changing it back again. If you do keep on fiddling, you may end up achieving very little, and worse still, you will have frittered and wasted money on early redemption charges and the like. Many investments are long term, and fiddling means paying more or not reaping the full benefits.

Sure, you should keep your eye on things and on the market generally, but stick with your strategy and, having done your homework, leave as well alone as possible. Don't panic and don't fiddle.

> ## ONCE YOU HAVE DECIDED TO LEAP, GET ON WITH IT.

RULE 54

Think Long Term

Just as you shouldn't fiddle too much (*see Rule 53*), so too you shouldn't play the short game. You have to think long term, both in your planning and in your expectations of a return. You also have to invest for the longer term.

If you expect a rapid and sudden catapult into prosperity, go play the lottery and good luck to you. (You'll need it.) Gaining wealth is a slow process, and rightly so. If you get it all quickly, you have no time to acquire experience and sense. Too quickly, and it'll be all "spend, spend, spend."

Thinking long term is a bit like thinking in very fast motion while the rest of the world moves incredibly slowly around you. *Easy does it,* as they say. Ever tried to swat a fly? A fly's eyes are different from ours and they basically see in fast forward. By the time you raise your hand, they have already predicted the movement and flown away. You have to develop the same ability. You have to see what's happening before it happens, and the only way to do that is to think long term.

Think of gaining prosperity as stalking a reluctant tiger. It'll be wary and cautious, and you have to stalk it skillfully, quietly, almost lovingly. It's no use running up and shouting at it—it will either turn round and kill you or run off. Better to take your time and creep up slowly and quietly. Any sudden movements will startle the canny beast.

> # THINK OF GAINING PROSPERITY AS STALKING A RELUCTANT TIGER.

In *The Rules of Work*, I talked about having various plans in force—short-term, medium-term, and long-term. The same is true for investments. You need short-term investments for money you might need access to in the near future; medium-term ones that you expect to deliver returns in five or ten years, and then you need long-term investments that will reap greater rewards but that deliver in the more distant future.

I know, in Rule 34, I said to be decisive and act quickly, and that is still true. But only after you have taken a long-term view; only after you have weighed and considered and pondered and evaluated. *The samurai only makes one cut, but that cut was an entire lifetime in the making.*

Where are you going to be in 5 years' time, prosperitywise? 10? 15? 20? Longer?

Have a Set Time of Day to Work on Your Wealth Strategy

You have to have a life as well as gaining prosperity. It is my observation that happy, wealthy people's financial planning follows a similar set of four principles:

- They set targets and then get on with it.
- They don't tinker too much.
- They tend to work on their financial planning at the same time of day. (I don't mean everyone works at, say, 9 a.m. but that each person tends to favor a particular time of day, whether it's 10:30 in the morning or midnight.)
- They can take a break from their financial planning and have a life outside it—it keeps them refreshed and interesting.

The reason you need a set time of day is twofold. First, it makes sure you actively manage your wealth rather than looking at it once a year and thinking "Oh dear," and conversely, it means you don't overdo it and spend all day tinkering (which as we've said is a bad idea). Second, it means you can take advantage of your natural biorhythms and put in the effort when you are at your brightest. If you are a morning person, you'll want to get your planning in early. If you are more of an owl, an evening slot will take advantage of your sharpest mental acuity.

The other big advantage of having a set time of day is that you can plan for it, work it into your calendar, and make time for it. If you don't, it can get forgotten or the time might be used for other things. If, for example, you always spend half an hour on your plan first thing after breakfast, then it gets to be a regular function and one you feel oddly uncomfortable missing—yes, even on vacation.

Working on your prosperity plan at the same time of day—and for the same short length of time—means you can break things down into manageable chunks and not get overwhelmed. You can work for a bit and then take a break, and put it behind you for the day and go back to it, at the same time, of course, the next day. Bit by bit, things will improve. Believe me, I've been here before you.

Pay Attention to Details

This is my biggest failing I'm afraid. My solution is easy. I employ someone to manage my life who takes care of the details—someone who is very, very good at the details. Yes, it's an expensive way to do it. It's better to train yourself right from the word go to pay attention to the details and save the expense.

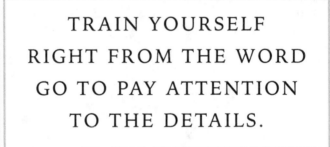

TRAIN YOURSELF RIGHT FROM THE WORD GO TO PAY ATTENTION TO THE DETAILS.

Details are not keeping notes of every tiny purchase you make and looking at minute economies. We've already discovered (*see Rule 32*) going without that cappuccino isn't going to make you rich beyond your wildest dreams. Details are

- Checking the small print
- Checking the interest rates
- Checking charges and fees
- Checking that you pay for things on time so that you don't incur penalties

- Checking when you will be paid and investing promptly to avoid your money lying idle
- Not forgetting people
- Not forgetting dates, times, and appointments
- Making lists and writing everything down
- Remembering to ask for information
- Remembering to ask questions in general
- Remembering to keep good records of all transactions, purchases, and sales

This is just muscle training. I take it you know all about muscle training? When you are in training for any sport, if you repeat an action often enough, your muscles retain the memory of that action. The more you repeat the action, the easier it gets, and the less effort you need to put in.

It's a bit like driving a car—tough at first, but it becomes automatic (excuse the pun!) after a while. I am writing this in France, and I have been getting used to (a) driving on the right and (b) driving a left-hand-drive car. I've had to concentrate hard and shout at the children, because I can't think if they are screaming in the back seat. It's been a bit like learning to drive all over again. Added to the fact that all the signs are in French and it's a steep learning curve. But it's getting easier and becoming routine. I don't have to think about it anymore and can take in the passing scenery and enjoy the journey.

Create New Income Streams

When it comes to wealth-creation strategies, investing wisely and managing your money actively are important, but nothing beats having more coming in the first place. Everybody benefits from some thought about where his income comes from and how he could create another source of revenue.

It's a bit like being a street musician and having good spots to play at. If one is proving unprofitable, you can pack it in and go somewhere else. But instead of packing it in, what you are going to do is duplicate yourself—a cloned you, if you like—and not only carry on playing on one street but also be playing in a new place at the same time. The more hats you have out, the more they are likely to return a profit.

Look, don't take my word for this. Check it out yourself. Look at any prosperous person you admire, and see if diversity isn't his tool for unlocking greater prosperity. The rich usually have several money-making schemes going for them.

This is especially important for anybody who loves his work but isn't paid well. What you need is another income stream.

There are a couple of ways of doing this. The first is to turn surplus cash into assets that will work for you and bring in income, even when you aren't there. Rent from a rental property would be one example, or annual dividends from shares you've bought.

The other way to create new income streams is to find ways of using your skills and expertise in more than one setting, so you aren't just swapping your labor for a paycheck in your day job.

This doesn't mean packing in your day job necessarily. It might mean, for example, doing some freelance work, either in the same area or a completely unrelated area where you also have skills and expertise. (Maybe you have a hobby, which means you have other skills and expertise that could be used?) Is there anything you could teach or consult on or that you could set up as a business?

When I say "create" new income streams, what I mean is create them *for you*. Just make sure that you are maximizing all your skills to bring in income and that you are actively investing in assets that will earn money for you without your having to be there. (I do realize you can't physically clone yourself.)

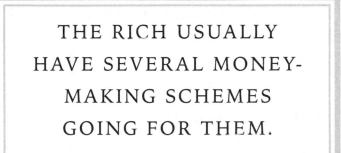

THE RICH USUALLY
HAVE SEVERAL MONEY-
MAKING SCHEMES
GOING FOR THEM.

Learn to Play "What If?"

When deciding how to earn your money and how to invest it, you need to ask yourself a lot of questions starting with "What if…?"

I'll start you off here:

- "What if there is another recession?"
- "What if this bank goes bust and I can't get my money out?"
- "What if these shares suddenly take a turn for the worse?"
- "What if gold prices plummet?"
- "What if all my customers went elsewhere for cheaper services/ products?"
- "What if I were no longer needed?"
- "What if property prices bottom out?"
- "What if the oil runs out?"

The "What if" game is one we can all play. All together now… "What if…?" I call it "looking for loopholes," only it isn't loopholes. It's more a sort of gotcha clause. Every time I start making some serious money, I figure someone somewhere is playing a gotcha clause whereby the unexpected happens and that particular income stream dries up rapidly. Part of the fun of being prosperous is in spotting the gotcha clause long before it happens and getting your money out and into another investment. It's also vital to consider when you are thinking about where to find extra income. That's where having lots of hats comes in.

A good example of the dangers of putting all your eggs in one basket are the football players who have been forced to retire while in their twenties. One minute they are earning millions and seemingly at the peak of their career, and then they shatter their ankle and their financial dreams, too. They haven't trained for anything else because it never occurred to them that they might need another string to their bow.

> ## DIVERSIFICATION IS THE
> ## NAME OF THE GAME.

Diversification is the name of the game. By having more than one income stream and a nice broad spread of investments, whatever happens in the "What if" scenario, you will be in a much more secure position than if you had all your proverbial eggs in one basket. By asking "What if…?" you are minimizing risks to your wealth and wealth creation.

Control Spending Impulses

The surest way to defeat your wealth creation is to go out and spend everything you earn or receive (and a bit more just for good measure). This particular addiction is very strong in me. I blame it all on giving up smoking. I have nothing to do now with my hands, so fiddling with a credit card seems to satisfy some deeply buried addictive urge. But you have to resist if you are going to turn what little you have into a bigger something. Forget notions of new cars and holidays in the sun. You are going to turn into a bit of a Scrooge for a while, hanging on to what you've got to prepare for the future when you will have so much more. This means you have to control your urges.

Look, I'm going to let you into a secret. Prosperity is a race, a prize, a winning line. We all set out wanting to race toward it, claim it. Some can't be bothered to even make it to the starting line because they are so weighed down with unhelpful beliefs that floor them before they start. And a whole lot of people fall by the wayside from laziness early on. A whole lot more fail to make the grade because they get daunted by the hard work needed. Still more, at this point, where you are now, stumble because they give into temptation and spend, spend, spend like there is no tomorrow.

Well, there is a tomorrow, and it comes quickly enough. And that shiny new car now looks sad and rusty, the holiday is gone with only a few photos of people and places you can't even remember, and the new clothes are outgrown and unworn.

The simple truth is that the rich know how to control their spending urges—that's why they're rich. When they need to tighten their belts, they can do it.

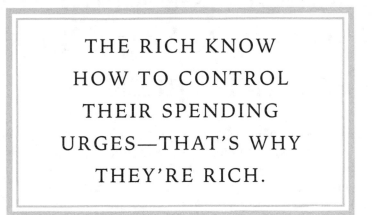

THE RICH KNOW
HOW TO CONTROL
THEIR SPENDING
URGES—THAT'S WHY
THEY'RE RICH.

You need to tighten your belt, too. In fact, what you need to do is not loosen it in the first place. We've talked about delayed pleasures in earlier Rules, and I hope you've absorbed that one by now. Curbing those spending urges is absolutely vital, and the best way to do it is to never buy anything instantly. If you see something you just have to have, wait a week. Do you still really need/want it? Chances are the urge will pass if you give it a chance to. Make it harder for yourself by putting time and distance between you and temptation.

Don't Answer Ads That Promise Get-Rich-Quick Schemes— It Won't Be You Who Gets Rich Quick

If you type in "Opportunities to make money" into Google, you get over 150,000,000 hits. That's not quite as many as "sex"[19] but still a pretty good indicator of what we want. There are a lot of get-rich-quick schemes in there. Now, believe me, they do work. What? I hear you cry. Yes, indeed, they do work. But not for you, not for the poor mugs who sign up. They work for the instigators, the beginners, the ones who launch such schemes.[20]

In the 1980s, there were a lot of water purifier selling schemes around. I was invited to a couple of their meetings and went along out of interest (strictly research, I promise). I was amazed at how quick people were to join in, to sign something, anything, that promised them loads of money with minimum effort. After all, what did they have to do but sell a water filter to a few friends and relations? Easy pickings, they all thought. Where are all the people now who signed up, invested their savings, were promised untold riches? Funny, I can't find any either.

Maybe a few did indeed sell some and alienated their loved ones in the process. Maybe there were a few at the beginning who did make quite a bit of money. But any pyramid scheme isn't sustainable and will collapse when it reaches a certain level because there just aren't enough people on the planet to sustain the promise.

---

[19] 688,000,000 if you Google "sex," but "God" is up there with 624,000,000, and "work" is a staggering 5,670,000,000, so maybe there's hope for us yet.
[20] 427,000 if you Google "get-rich-quick schemes."

I like what Woody Allen says about a fool and his money—how did they get together in the first place?[21]

> ## A FOOL AND HIS MONEY—HOW DID THEY GET TOGETHER IN THE FIRST PLACE?

When I was a kid, I remember reading about a couple of scams that set me thinking about how gullible people are. The first was a pest killer. You sent off $5 to buy a pest killer guaranteed to kill any household pest, including fleas, cockroaches, mice, and so on. What you got back were two small blocks of wood with the instruction to catch and place the pest on block A and then press down block B with great force. I kid you not. And the perpetrators made a lot of money before they got caught. Might be time to try that one again. The second scam was someone offering a yard of silk during a silk crisis for a similar small fee (notice how the amount is always small enough to tempt you in), and what you got back was a yard of silk thread—they had never specified the width.

Now, you might be thinking you are too clever to be taken in by such obvious hoaxes. Yes? Well, they aren't all as obvious, and you might not believe the schemes that otherwise very smart people sign up to. There are no get-rich-quick schemes. Repeat after me: There are no....

---

[21] It may not have been Woody Allen, of course—he does get a lot of quotes attributed to him, especially cynical ones about money and God. Woody also said—and it was definitely him this time—that money was better than poverty if only for financial reasons.

There Are No Secrets

Just as there are no get-rich-quick schemes, there also are no secrets—so don't go buying any of them either. You will be offered loads. After your attention is focused on becoming prosperous, all sorts of offers are going to come at you out of the woodwork. And they'll all offer to let you in on the secrets only the really rich know.

You'll get offered very expensive newsletters that will tell you the hidden secrets of Wall Street, how to play the stock exchange and win, how to invest and make a fortune, and how to move your money around in offshore accounts to avoid paying taxes. And it'll cost you so little! All you've got to do is sign up for 12 monthly issues.

Guess what? The only secret being sold is the one that says there's a sucker born every minute. And now that you know that secret, you, too, can just say no. No one but you is going to make you wealthy. No one in the whole wide world. They don't know more than you. They don't have access to any more information than you do.

> # NO ONE BUT YOU IS GOING TO MAKE YOU WEALTHY. NO ONE IN THE WHOLE WIDE WORLD.

The secret of making money is that there are no secrets. You buy something, and if you sell it for more than you paid, you've done well. And that applies to anything and everything in the financial world—stocks and shares and investments and property portfolios and IRAs and budget funds and finance management and commodity futures and gold reserves and conch shells.

One of the earliest rules we had to learn was that only industrious people can be prosperous. Can you see why now? You have to put in a bit of effort to learn how to do it by studying the wealthy. If you think there are shortcuts, like buying get-rich-quick schemes or buying secrets, not only are you going to be disappointed, but you'll also be worse off than if you hadn't invested in such nonsense. Lazy people not only don't get rich, but they also often end up poorer because they look for such shortcuts.

Don't Just Read This—Do Something

I'm afraid it's time to shift some weight off that backside and actually do something. Reading this book is a start, but it'll count for nothing unless you actually take action. You've probably thought to yourself while reading this book "Oh I know that!" or "That's so obvious…." Okay, you know it, but have you actually done something about it? Sure, parts are obvious, but does that mean you've got it sorted? For most of us, there is a huge gap between what we know and what we do. There's no point just reading this—you have to act on whatever it spurs you to think would be a good idea.

Let's take it as slowly as you want. I do appreciate that changing direction is often hard; developing new character traits can be painful. Begin by changing what you watch and what you read. Begin by simply reading/watching a bit of business news. Begin by changing your awareness of what money is all about and how our money myths influence every interaction we have with it.

> ## CHANGING DIRECTION IS OFTEN HARD; DEVELOPING NEW CHARACTER TRAITS CAN BE PAINFUL.

The way to change our mindset is to change the way we behave and the way we conduct ourselves.

- Watch how you talk, and think, about money. Do you praise its many virtues or denigrate it as something evil and negative? If you begin to talk it up, you'll be surprised how quickly it materializes.

- Watch how you walk. Do you slouch and give off an air of resigned acceptance? Or are you upright and confident and looking as if you are hungry for change? (*See also Rule 22.*)

- Watch your overall image, too. Plead poverty all the time, and people will assume you are poor and act accordingly. The best thing to do is to "act as if" you are already rich, and people will adjust their perception of you and reaction to you accordingly.

Many people will fall by the wayside, despite claiming they want to be rich or richer, but they will do so not from a lack of desire. Instead, it will be from a lack of motivation, a lack of doing something. Start now, right now, today, immediately.

PART III

GETTING EVEN WEALTHIER

After you get a bit of money behind you, the entire thing gets a bit easier. Money begets money. You won't pick up a lot of bargains at an antiques auction for $50. But there's a hell of a lot more if you've got $5,000. It's that first million that is difficult—ho ho. But seriously, after you start to move toward prosperity, it isn't a good idea to sit back and start counting your loot. It'll disappear faster that way than by any other means. Instead, you've got to get slicker and quicker, stay on your toes, be even busier and more focused, and definitely don't take your eye off the ball.

As you start to get richer, you might need to start gathering a few advisers around you, people you can trust and, most importantly, listen to. The reason? Because as your investments and capital start to grow, you will need advice and help to make things grow even more. Obviously, you can listen, but you will need to make the final decisions about what you are going to do.

Not sitting back on your laurels means you have to be on the lookout for hidden opportunities to take your prosperity further. You've got to stay abreast of current developments, play your hunches, understand the market, and know what you've got and what you can spend/invest/save.

Now is the time to start stepping up how opportunistic you can be—thinking laterally, not following the herd, being creative and innovative. There's no point in doing what everyone else does if you want to make some serious money.

Carry Out a Finance Health Check Regularly

It is essential if you are going to increase your prosperity that you maintain a healthy awareness of your bank balance. You should be carrying out a finance health check on a regular basis. I think it should be weekly. Of course, you are free to do it as often as you want, and if that means monthly or even longer, then that is entirely up to you, but I wouldn't recommend that you leave it too long.

My observation is that the tighter a grip you have on the pulse of your financial life

- The quicker you can react to changes
- The more information you have to make decisions
- The less chance there is for things to go drastically wrong without your noticing
- The better a focus—and thus interest—you'll have in your finances

Sorry, but you do have to be disciplined about this. You have to have a regular time when you sit down and

- Carry out a bank reconciliation
- List your creditors and debtors
- Check credit card balances against receipts
- Check outstanding checks—the ones that you've written that haven't yet arrived in the bank
- Check what future income you have and what major expenses you might have looming on the horizon

- Check your standing orders
- Check pension contributions
- Check investments
- Check any loans
- Check any overdrafts, etc. (I know, I know, I have said not to have any, but you are human.)

If you don't do this stuff, money will leak away. Forgetting a debt doesn't pay it.

> # FORGETTING A DEBT
> # DOESN'T PAY IT.

You've got to be disciplined and have a routine—every Monday morning without fail. Yep, even when it's sunny outside, even on vacation, even when you're feeling a bit off-color, even when there are more exciting things going on. Because if this doesn't excite you, then you're not going to make it, I'm afraid.

I think you should know what you are earning every day by the day. And you should know what big outgoings you might face in the next 12 months, and that does include a most often forgotten one—the IRS payment. Watch that little baby like a hawk, and never take your eyes off that ball, because it will get you every time.

Get Some Money Mentors

When not writing books, I do have a proper job. I have several, in fact, which all involve running companies. I'm no fool when it comes to knowledge. I know there are things I should know that I don't know. And there must be millions of things I don't even know I don't know. My solution is to use other people's knowledge to supplement my own deficits. I have money mentors. In fact, I have mentors for all sorts of situations, but we'll stick to the money ones for the moment.

Now, why should you use money mentors?

- They bring a wider range of experience to the table.
- They make you present your ideas in a clear and concise format, which makes you think long and hard about what you are doing.
- They will make you justify what you are doing, which makes it much harder for you to go off like a loose cannon.
- They are on tap to provide answers, advice, as a sounding platform, a reigning-in service, and a "Have you thought it through?" facility.
- They will individually keep their ear to the ground so that you can benefit from their collective knowledge (a bit like a news-gathering service).
- They are independent, so they will have no vested interest in what you do as competition.
- They are independent and thus will be loyal, supportive, and on your team.

Many successful entrepreneurs use mentors when they start out in business. They find somebody who has been successful in starting and running his own businesses, and they ask if this person would be prepared to offer guidance and advice (and sometimes contacts and more) to the new entrepreneur as he starts out. The vast majority of experienced businesspeople approached will say yes—it's fun for them to pass on their expertise. They enjoy it.

Yes, but I have questions, I hear you say. Fire away.

- What sort of mentor do I need?
- Where do I find one?
- What's it going to cost me?
- Can I ignore a mentor if I don't agree with his advice?

For money mentors, you need people who have proven their financial acumen by making a bit of money themselves—and not by inheritance or lottery winnings. You find them by looking around you. Approach anyone you admire who has been successful—they may well be flattered.

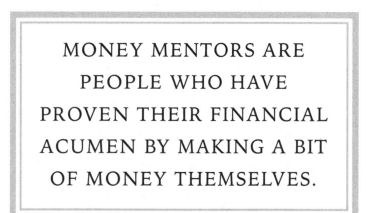

MONEY MENTORS ARE PEOPLE WHO HAVE PROVEN THEIR FINANCIAL ACUMEN BY MAKING A BIT OF MONEY THEMSELVES.

It shouldn't cost you more than about four decent lunches a year. You take them out to lunch. In return, they give you advice, information, suggestions, restraint, support, and encouragement.

And can you ignore what they say if you don't like it? Yes, of course you can. I ignored mine once. Just once. It cost me a lot to ignore them. I publicly apologized to them and would never ignore them again.

Play Your Hunches

Have a hunch. Listen to your heart. Follow your intuition. Listen to your inner voice. Have a gut feeling. Have an inkling. These are all saying the same thing. There are times when

- You know something stinks
- You know when something is absolutely right
- You need to nod your head and believe in yourself

Of course, having a hunch, following a hunch, and going off like a loose cannon are not all the same thing.

> OF COURSE, HAVING A HUNCH, FOLLOWING A HUNCH, AND GOING OFF LIKE A LOOSE CANNON ARE NOT ALL THE SAME THING.

RULE 65

There is a format to this intuition mischief, and it is a little bit more sensible than you'd think:

- Have the hunch.
- Do your research and see if your hunch is worth following—it usually is, but it's best to check first.
- Prepare a well-worked proposal to present to your money mentors.
- Present.
- Listen and act on their advice.

And there is no point whining, "But I had this really brilliant hunch!" If you can't back up your hunch with facts and figures, then it is just a stab in the dark. A hunch is a sudden flash of inspiration, a moment of sublime intuition, a clever and brilliant realization. And these all can be justified with facts and figures. Just because the inspiration was a hunch doesn't mean you don't have to justify it and research it. You still need to prepare some figures and develop a plan. Having a hunch doesn't let you off being sensible, practical, and realistic.

Lots of wealthy people got there by having that one truly brilliant moment of inspiration. They then turned that inspiration into perspiration (sorry) and worked their guts out to make their dream come true. I bet loads of people said to them, "But you're so lucky." Bah. No such thing as luck. But there is such a thing a hunch followed by hard work.

Don't Sit Back

There's a saying that "Nothing wilts faster than laurels that have been rested upon." It's very true. There is a temptation once we have made a bit of money, when an investment has worked out, or it seems to be all paying off, to sit back and relax. Yes, we can. But we don't want to. Now is the time to speed up a gear or two, put more irons in the fire. Now is the time to look around and work out our next plan of attack. Now is the time to strike, capitalize, and consolidate. Now is not the time to take our eye off the ball.

> ## NOW IS THE TIME TO STRIKE, CAPITALIZE, AND CONSOLIDATE.

We can all stir from the swamp and then settle back into the mud. But the really prosperous keep struggling until they are completely free of the slime forever. If you take a day off, the slide begins and will, inexorably, continue. And the next effort will be even harder. I know. I've been there.

So, redouble your efforts. Rekindle the enthusiasm. Relight the fires of desire, and let's get back to work.

RULE 66

You mustn't sit back. The wealthy don't take days off, tea breaks, lunch breaks, or vacations. They keep their nose to the grindstone, shoulder to the wheel, ear to the ground, back to the wall, finger on the pulse, iron in the fire, fire in their belly, and hand on the tiller. Wow! Tall order. They work harder and enjoy greater rewards—and get told how lucky they are.

You've got to keep on doing whatever it was that made you make it. If it's a cash cow, ride that baby until it dies under you. If it was a one-off brainwave, have another. If it was sheer hard work, keep going. If you've found a successful formula, make some more. But whatever you do, don't turn off the tap unless it's run dry. Even then, keep it turned on just in case.

Remember, don't get clever. Don't think you know it all. Keep using those money mentors. Keep working harder than anyone around you. Keep it under your hat, and keep at it.

But don't forget how you got to where you are—location, method, plan, mission. Remember the "Don't fiddle" rule, and don't change anything until you are sure it will only improve results and not make the boat sink.

Get Someone to Do the Stuff You Can't

I have money mentors because there are loads of stuff to do with business and making money that I know nothing about. There are also loads of things that have to be done that I don't know how to do. I could learn, but it isn't where my talents lie. So why go learning how to do things when there are eminently more suitable people out there who can do them? Do what you are good at, and get others to do the things you can't. Simple. Pick really good people, and let them get on with the job of making you really prosperous.

Now, there are ten rules to making sure you (a) get the right people and (b) keep the right people:

1 Know exactly what it is you want done and who you want to do it.

2 Be very clear about what you want them to do for you, how much you will pay, and what guidelines you will give them.

3 Care about them—they are human and mustn't become a mere tool.

4 Keep them informed and motivated—inspire loyalty.

5 Tell them your long-term strategy—they, too, have a stake in your/their future.

6 If they muck up—and they will from time to time, we all do (even you, Mr. Templar? Well, maybe not me)—then correct it and move on. Forgiveness is a good thing.

7 Praise them constantly—nothing inspires more than praise (besides money, of course).

> PICK REALLY GOOD
> PEOPLE, AND LET THEM
> GET ON WITH THE JOB
> OF MAKING YOU REALLY
> PROSPEROUS.

8 Set realistic targets, but don't expect the impossible.

9 Set a good example—be someone they can respect and look up to (no one likes working for a jerk)—and set high standards and live up to them yourself.

10 Remember, you're the boss, not their friend. Try to maintain dignity, distance, and authority.

That should do it. There may be other things you will try, adapt, implement, and use. All this stuff is adaptable and entirely up to you. Just make sure you treat your people well and have fun. Don't be an insensitive bossy boss—as if!

At the moment, I have a wonderful accounts person. She sighs a lot because I'm always trying to find ways to ensure I'm not paying more tax than I need to—don't we all? But all I do is ask her questions. The rest I leave entirely up to her, and the relationship works. Apart from the sighing, that is.

Know Yourself—Solo, Duo, or Team Player

If you are going to change direction—in this case to prosperity from wherever it is you are now—then you need to know

- Your strengths and weaknesses
- What you are good at—and bad at, obviously (and this isn't the same as strengths and weaknesses)

For example, I'm good at broad strokes, big picture stuff, but I'm not the greatest when it comes to detail.

Get what I'm talking about? You just have to know yourself pretty well, and then you will be confident in the areas you are good at, can brush up in areas you are weak, can trade on your strengths, and can get someone else to do all the stuff you are bad at (or haven't yet learned or researched or studied).

Then you've got to know if you are at your best working as part of a partnership, a team, or alone. I always need the steadying hand of a partner to curb some of my business excesses— an overwhelming tendency to shoot from the hip, be a bit undiplomatic at times, rush headlong into things, spend money wastefully on advertising, and not attend to detail. I am, however, really bad in a team of more than two. So, if a business opportunity comes up that requires teamwork, I know I can turn it down or tailor it in some way, because I know if I say yes, I will make a pig's ear of it. If, however, it requires a partnership, I'm much more likely to be interested.

> ## I ALWAYS NEED THE STEADYING HAND OF A PARTNER TO CURB SOME OF MY BUSINESS EXCESSES.

I am also good working alone. I make decisions easily (not always the right ones, but at least I don't procrastinate), I am happy in my own company for long periods, and I don't need to bounce ideas off anyone to make them seem real. I can travel well alone and can speak up for myself. See what I mean about knowing yourself?

You have to do this exercise if you are to forge ahead with the rest of the moneymakers. Questions to ask:

- Am I good on my own, or do I need other people around me?
- Do I have a role to play in a team and feel happier in that role?
- Can I work well with just one trusted partner?
- Do I know where my strengths and weaknesses are, and do I know the difference?
- Do I know what I am good and bad at?

My business partner says we work well together because we are the "brains and brawn." The only trouble is we both see ourselves as the brains and the other as the brawn. Oh well.

Look for the Hidden Asset/Opportunity

You've got to be a vigilant, never-sleeping, never-taking-time-off machine. Always alert, always on the lookout for that opportunity. An old Senegalese proverb says that the opportunities that God sends do not wake up those who are asleep. Wake up! Sleep is for the lazy, the indolent, the poor. Wide awake, restless, prowling is for the hungry, the lean, the opportunity taker, the rich. All around us all of the time there are opportunities to make a fortune. All we have to do is be open to the possibilities, to the magic of such events.

There are only five things you need to take on board if you are going to be a treasure seeker:

1 **Timing is crucial.** React too slowly, and the opportunity is gone. Too fast, and you might startle it. Markets shift, fashions change, and products fade.

2 **You have to be serious.** There is no point in being on the ball every other day or only in the mornings. Hidden opportunities reveal themselves only when they feel they want to. I always imagine them as small, shy beasts coming down to the waterhole for a drink. If you want to catch one, you have to creep up really quietly, really skillfully.

3 **You have to be quirky.** If there are only a few hidden opportunities, you need to stand out. Quirky, unique, special, creative, unusual—name it however you will, but you have to stand out from the herd (to complete the animal analogy).

4 **You've got to know what you're doing.** Wealth, like any other skill, needs to be learned. To spot opportunities and to take advantage of them, you need to give yourself the best chance. You can't pick up a financial paper and say you are going to

understand it from Day 1. It takes time, dedication, and commitment. Know your stuff, and you'll see the opportunities much more clearly. There's a management technique called "SWOT anaylsis"—an acronym for "strengths, weaknesses, opportunites, and threats"—keep looking at all four.

5 **Be attractive.** If you smell horrid, that shy beast is going to bolt. You have to dress smartly, smell fresh, look good, be well turned out, and radiate attractiveness.

All around us all of the time there are opportunities to make a fortune. All we have to do is be open to the possibilities, to the magic of such events.

Have you ever noticed that when you are thinking of changing cars to another make or model, you immediately start noticing hundreds of that make on the roads? Were they there before? Of course. It's just that you never noticed them. But once your attention is focused like a narrow beam of intense light, it throws them into sharp focus.

Opportunities are a bit like that. When we start noticing them, they are all around us. We just need that kick-start, that beginning of the search. Just like changing cars, we change our focus.

It is essential that we wake up our opportunity detector. When we do, they will appear as if by magic all around us.

> # THE OPPORTUNITIES GOD SENDS DO NOT WAKE UP THOSE WHO ARE ASLEEP.

Don't Try to Get Rich Too Quickly

We've already said you need to think long term. Trying to get rich quick leads only to disappointment and over-anxious hustling. And you do need to build a good base, or your financial castle can topple at the first gust of wind. The longer you take to make your money, the more diverse you'll be with investments and income streams.

The quicker you make your money, the more likely it'll be a single strand and thus easy to break.

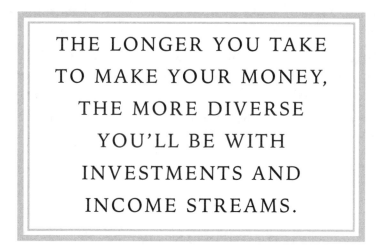

THE LONGER YOU TAKE TO MAKE YOUR MONEY, THE MORE DIVERSE YOU'LL BE WITH INVESTMENTS AND INCOME STREAMS.

Getting rich over time usually means you'll

- Build long-term income streams
- Be insured against recession or sudden and negative market downturns

- Have time to have a life as well—that old work/home relationship is less likely to be fractured
- Be better at making money honestly and decently
- Have time to make the relevant adjustments and thus not so likely to rush out and spend inappropriately
- Gain the experience necessary for long-term financial security as you go along

If you make your money too quickly, there is a tendency to

- Spend it inappropriately
- Not have time to learn to handle it well
- Risk losing it by having your income coming from one area only

If you really do want to earn a lot quickly, you might like to take a leaf out of 81-year-old Stella Liebeck's book. She sued McDonald's because she burned herself with spilled hot coffee and was awarded initially $2.9 million—later knocked down to a mere $640,000.

This may not have been a deliberate game plan, but it did pay off—and quickly. I would rather make my money slowly and enjoyably and not have to sue anyone to get it—or win the lottery, or have a close relative die, or have to marry someone inappropriate merely because she had a dollar or two. Make your money slowly, and you'll enjoy it more. It will last longer, and you'll sleep nights.

Always Ask What's in It for Them

I don't want you to be paranoid generally, but it is okay to be paranoid when it comes to your money. There are a lot of sharks out there looking for easy pickings from the less awake among us. Watch out.

Think of any of a half dozen broadcasters who always interview politicians with a basic underlying assumption that they are hiding something and they have to find out what and why.

Obviously, we don't want to go round believing everybody is out to get us, but there is a good technique here that we can adopt to question anyone

- Offering us a money-making proposition
- Offering to "look after" our money
- Looking to invest in our future or schemes
- Offering us any financial advice
- Offering to work for us
- Offering us a partnership
- Offering us products or services

You have to be suspicious of anyone and anything that could make inroads into your wealth. Be very wary of anybody who

- Promises to help you get rich quick by short-cuts, use of tax loopholes, or dubiously legal schemes
- Uses the word "offshore"
- Uses pyramid selling

- Claims to be incredibly wealthy and is offering to share his secrets with you—the secret is he makes his money out of people like you (*see Rule 61*)
- Offers to increase your wealth by using the Internet
- Asks for money upfront to seed investment, pay for promotional material, or carry out a survey

And three things to always remember:

- If it waddles like a duck and quacks like a duck, then it is a duck, and don't let anyone tell you it isn't.
- If it looks too good to be true, it probably is.
- Not all that glitters is gold.

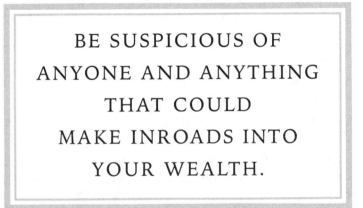

BE SUSPICIOUS OF ANYONE AND ANYTHING THAT COULD MAKE INROADS INTO YOUR WEALTH.

Remember also to keep asking, "What's in it for this person?" Don't trust anyone. Don't give your money to anyone to look after for you. Check the small print of anything you sign. Be on your guard.

RULE 72

Make Your Money Work for You

An awful lot of us are guilty of wasting money by not making the best use of it—whether it's a small amount or large, long term or short term. This waste includes everything from not cashing checks to leaving cash in low-interest accounts because we've forgotten about it or can't find the time or be bothered to move it.

Here are a few tips to get you thinking about whether you are making all your money work for you:

- Don't leave money inactive in bank accounts—move it around to high-interest accounts, even if it's only for a few days. Electronic banking means money can be easily and simply switched from one account to another—even for very short periods.

- Never be satisfied with the interest rate you are getting—there's always a better one out there. Keep actively looking.

- Shop around for all services you pay for. There are always cheaper options. Don't just pay for a name—pay for what you are getting.

- Don't leave property empty—it may be increasing in value, but you are missing valuable rental income.

- If you invest in anything that is appreciating in value, could it also be useful? Would a classic car you can drive be more useful to you as opposed to a painting you can only look at. (Although that could be regarded as useful in the sense it might be relaxing or therapeutic, but let's not go there.)

RULE 72

- Explore all options. Never be content with what you are doing, but always be on the lookout for ways to improve, enhance, perk up, progress, and advance. This does not mean fiddling, of course.
- Move on. Don't put anything off for tomorrow. Do it today. Do it now. If you take four months to bank a check, that's four months interest you've lost.
- Always remember that idle money is wasted money—use it or lose it.

> ## NEVER BE SATISFIED WITH THE INTEREST RATE YOU ARE GETTING.

Know When to Let Go of Investments

I have my own little calculation about when to let go, and I am happy to pass it on to you. I learned it from an Internet site a while back, and it has stood me in good stead. Basically, for an investment to work for me means I am looking for a return that will double my money in five years.

The calculation I use is to divide the interest rate into 72 to find out how long it will take me to double my money. For example, if the interest rate on a particular investment is 6 percent, then it will take me 12 years (72 ÷ 6 = 12) to double my money. Too long for me. So I would be looking for an interest rate (known as a "return") of around 14.4 percent. (I know, I know, you'd be lucky at the moment, but this is only an example.) This works for any amount of money incidentally.

So, if you want to know what interest rate to look for, divide 72 by the number of years you are prepared to wait. 72 ÷ 5 = 14.4%. Gosh, something useful for you there, and I did all the work for you.

For me, therefore, any investment that looks like it won't double my money in five years I pass on, or if it makes financial sense to get out (i.e., no penalty for doing so), I will let go of. I have my criteria. You need yours.

Perhaps you need to let go when

- You feel in your gut that something is not right.
- The market has taken a downturn.

- You read something that makes you curious or suspicious of a particular investment.
- You need the money for something better, hotter.
- The investment hasn't been doing well for a while and is sluggish.
- You've achieved your maximum profit and it's time to get out.
- You've lost interest in a particular investment and simply can't be bothered anymore.
- You have changed emotionally or ideologically and need to move on—perhaps you only invested environmentally and now want mainstream or vice versa.
- The investment isn't fashionable any more—old hat can be costly if the return isn't there.
- You need to spread your portfolio around to minimize losses in a recession or down market.
- You bought blind and now have more information—and can see your fingers getting burned.
- Throwing good money after bad will just aggravate the situation. Cut your losses and get out. (*See Rule 74.*)

> ## PERHAPS YOU ONLY INVESTED ENVIRONMENTALLY AND NOW WANT MAINSTREAM OR VICE VERSA.

There's a Chinese proverb: "The more you know, the more luck you have." So it is that the more money you gain, the more knowledge of the markets you'll need. Take it slowly and build a portfolio based on experience, knowledge, decent advice, up-to-date research, and helpful friends. And if an investment isn't working, know when to let it go.

I know a man who bought shares in his company when he worked there—a good investment at the time because he bought them at a discount as an employee perk. After he left the company, he found out from contacts that the company was beginning to get into trouble and read about industry changes that he knew would be bad for the company. Sadly, he was too lazy to do anything about his shares and didn't sell when there was the first sniff that all wasn't well. The value of these shares is now half of what it was. He knew when to let go, but he didn't do it.

Don't Chase Bad Luck Runs

We all have a tendency to buy based on tips from others, to buy on a whim, to buy glamorous, to invest too much in any one thing, to ride a winner to death, and most fatally of all, we fail to quit a loser. This is one thing we really need to let go of.

We all have a tendency to buy based on tips from others, to buy on a whim, to buy glamorous, to invest too much in any one thing, to ride a winner to death, and most fatally of all, we fail to quit a loser. This is one thing we really need to let go of.

Just as we experience various driving styles out on the highway, ranging from competitively aggressive to those unprepared to even be on the road, investors fall into some of the same patterns. Recognizing some of the basic investment styles lets us find out more about our own styles. Consider four basic styles, based on the experiences of Merrill Lynch[22]:

- **The Aggressive Investor**. Competitive, and a mostly male group, these charge out early with a lot of energy. They know about their investments, but their greed and over-confidence encourage them to chase a losing streak.

- **The Careful Investor**. A good third of all investors, this group has only slightly more males than females. They see the big picture and think in terms of long-term goals. The one thing wrong with this is that they have a hard time letting go, which leads them to chase a losing streak, too.

- **The Overly Cautious Investor**. The majority here is slightly to the female side of the ledger, and they are prone to listen to advisors. Often they wait too long to invest, and they can let go

---

[22] www.ml.com/?id=7695_7696_8149_46028_47486_47543

quicker than any of the other types. When it comes right down to it, they don't really enjoy investing.

- **The Totally Unready Investor**. Only a little more than 10% of all investors, and again slightly with more females than male in this group, they are timid about the whole idea, slow to get going, invest too little, and hardly ever let go in time. Hot tips weigh as much as due diligence to this group, which is in part why the experience often is not fun.

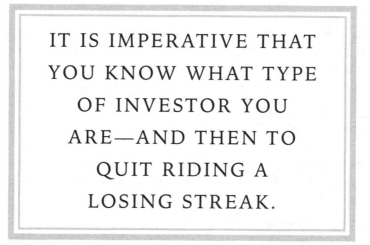

> IT IS IMPERATIVE THAT YOU KNOW WHAT TYPE OF INVESTOR YOU ARE—AND THEN TO QUIT RIDING A LOSING STREAK.

The point is that money carries an emotional value for all of us, and the quicker we get a grip on our own tendencies in respect to investment, the better able we can head off disasters and get out of dilemmas.

It is imperative that you know what type of investor you are— and then to quit riding a losing streak. Nothing clouds your judgment more than throwing good money after bad. You have to learn to cut your losses and walk away. And yes, I do know how hard that can be.

Know Why You Should Be Able to Read a Balance Sheet—and How

If you are going to run a company or invest in companies, you need to be able to read a balance sheet. This is different from knowing what profit or loss a company has made (i.e., reading a profit and loss account). Why? Because a profit and loss account only shows you half the picture.

For instance, Company X might have a turnover of $1 million and expenses of $500,000; thus, it has made a profit of $500,000 and must be doing really well, *n'est-ce pas*? No, actually. Because what you can't see from this simple profit and loss account is that it owes the bank $2 million, the $1 million in turnover is very unreliable, and there is a $4 million tax bill hanging over its head from previous years' accounts, a franchise expiring, tax loophole about to close, and a powerful competitor about to start up. Invest in Company X? I don't think so. It's bankrupt and fraudulently trading and is not worth a pig's ear. Stay away. So you need to see a balance sheet—without fail—because of what it is *not* telling you.

A balance sheet has to balance. That's why it's called a balance sheet.[23] The basic formula you need to know is Assets minus Liabilities = Equity, or A − B = C. Into even simpler terms: What you own less what you owe equals what you are worth. This applies to yourself, companies you work for/own, and companies you intend to invest in.

---

[23] The actual balance is Equity + Liabilities = Assets, thus balancing. You get assets on one side and liabilities and equity on the other.

RULE 75

A BALANCE SHEET HAS TO BALANCE.

Let's have a closer look:

- **A: What you own—your assets.** This is made up of current assets, including cash and anything that can be realized (i.e. turned into cash) within, say, a three-month period (this might include cast-iron debtors, money in transit, etc.); stock (stuff ready to be sold and raw materials that have value and can be made into products); any property you or the company may own; and equipment and goodwill.

- **B: What you owe—your liabilities.** This includes your creditors, long-term loans, and bank loans. Basically, what you would have to find in cash if everyone called in what you owed them.

- **C: What you are worth—your equity.** This is A minus B. It tells us what you or your company is actually worth. There is a formula that says that you take your current assets and divide it by your liabilities, and if the answer is bigger than 1.5, you're doing okay. Obviously, you need to adjust this for different industries and businesses, but it serves as a basic indicator. I also take the equity and divide it by the assets as a percentage. And if the answer is higher than 50, I feel confident. For instance, equity 35 million ÷ by assets (capital employed) of 70 million as a percentage = 35,000,000 ÷ 70,000,000% = 50, which is fine. But assets of 120 million and equity of 35 million is not so hot—around 29.

So, if you just hear about a company that has made a profit of $1 million and are offered the chance to invest, don't be impressed by that single figure. Ask to see the balance sheet. Read it thoroughly. In fact, don't just read the balance sheet, important as it is. There are other things you need to know, such as a company's financial statements in total. The more information you can get (and should get), the more solid your decision will be.

Be One Step Ahead of Your Tax Collector

You must never try to evade paying your taxes. If you do, you will go to prison—and quite rightly so. No, I am not on the side of the tax collector. There's a difference here between evade (criminal) and avoid (sensible). There is a line between making sure you aren't giving money unnecessarily to the tax collector—avoiding—and deliberately evading tax illegitimately. Cross that line at your peril. But there should be no need to do so. There are many good people out there who will give you all the advice you need.

> THERE ARE MANY GOOD PEOPLE OUT THERE WHO WILL GIVE YOU ALL THE ADVICE YOU NEED.

The more money you have, the greater the need to avoid tax—I stress this is not the same thing at all as evading—and the more expensive it becomes to do so. Obviously, there is a tipping point whereby you are obliged to hand over your tax affairs to experts—who naturally cost an arm and leg—so you can avoid paying the tax collectors the other arm and leg you have left.

As you move up the prosperity ladder, the tax issues get more complex. And there are all sorts of options. But remember the tax collectors are closing loopholes, changing laws, cutting off avenues as fast as you and your expensive experts can devise ways of avoiding tax. It's like a chess game, only much more exciting and expensive.

I am not going to give you specific advice, because it changes too quickly and I don't want to get sued, but areas worth bearing in mind are

- Consider establishing a Limited Company—it can attract less tax and give you all sorts of options not available to the "self-employed." I'm assuming you are making some money—if you aren't, there is obviously no tax to save as there is no tax to pay.
- Always make sure you make full use of your allowances—use them or lose them.
- Always consider if something is tax deductible before you buy it.
- Become a resident in a tax haven—but be quick because they are being shut down fast.
- Invest heavily in your own pension fund—it's tax free—or as about tax free as you can get these days.
- Become a tax nomad and wander the world not paying tax anywhere—watch out since there are circumstances when you can be based abroad but still pay tax. (It depends on residency—ordinarily residency and domicile.)

And, of course, make sure you are well up on investments that you don't have to pay tax on. Get good advice, and be willing to pay for good advice.

Learn How to Make Your Assets Work for You

First off, do you know what assets you have? You need to include both long-term assets (fixed assets) and short-term assets (current assets). The fixed assets are the ones it would take you a while to turn into cash, and the current assets are the ones easily converted into cash. Have you listed them? If not, do so now. I'll wait.

Back already? Got your list? I hope it has some of the following on it:

- Property
- Land
- Motor vehicles
- Pension funds
- Cash
- Goodwill
- Works of art, antiques, etc.
- Investments
- Money owed
- Furniture and other possessions
- Patents
- Stocks and bonds
- Intellectual properties

If you have a business, it may also include things like

- Stock
- Work in progress

- Raw materials
- Plant and machinery
- Equipment
- Trademarks
- Mailing lists

After you start writing your assets down as a list, you begin to see endless possibilities for using them to make more money. Basically, the personal advice is

- Don't let an asset sit idle. If you own property, rent it out. And I don't just mean buy-to-lease. Some enterprising people have rented garages or small bits of land they don't use in areas where there isn't enough parking for commuters and so on. Think laterally, and don't discount anything!
- No asset is beautiful unless it is working for you. It has to be accumulating, increasing in value, to be worth keeping.
- Never leave cash sitting around. It tends to get bored and wander off. Make it work.

> YOU BEGIN TO SEE
> ENDLESS POSSIBILITIES
> FOR USING ASSETS TO
> MAKE MORE MONEY.

And on top of those, the business advice is

- Keep stock and raw materials to a minimum—more is less.
- Depreciation is a dirty word. Keep its use to a minimum, and then excuse yourself every time you use it. But if you don't depreciate equipment, you are fooling yourself about net worth.
- If you own something, borrow against it to buy more and then borrow against that to expand further. All businesses are expanding or contracting. They are like plants, flourishing and growing or wilting and dying—you choose. (I know I said earlier not to borrow, but you can borrow against assets. Just don't borrow for revenue expenditure.)
- It is a false economy to extend the life of plant or equipment past its safe-to-use date. The legal ramifications are enormous.
- Don't give more credit than you need to. Money owed is money wasted.
- Chase debtors.

Never Believe You're Worth Only What You're Being Paid

Those who believe they are worth only what an employer pays them are almost always selling themselves short. Big companies depend on people not questioning their worth. Don't let them get away with it.

There are several points here. First, it's a fact that if you work for an employer, those who change their jobs fairly frequently tend to get pay rises each time and, therefore, end up earning more than those who stay with the same company (maybe for very good reasons, like being happy). If you are staying put, you have to learn to ask for more and demonstrate how you are adding value to an organization to justify being paid more.

Second, no company is ever going to pay more for anything than it really has to. You need to be proactive and ask for more, and show you are worth more. It requires you to take action, however. Don't wait to be recognized. If you are freelance, the same applies. Nobody will suddenly offer to pay you more for your work—you need to be proactive and show you are worth more.

Third, if you think you are always worth more, it makes you restless, ambitious, and keen to get on. If you accept what is offered and never question it, then it makes you complacent, and you'll get taken for granted.

> # IF YOU THINK YOU ARE ALWAYS WORTH MORE IT MAKES YOU RESTLESS, AMBITIOUS, AND KEEN TO GET ON.

Now, this is not a book about how to get a pay raise,[24] but here are a few tips:

- Don't accept that you are worth only what they are paying you—that's always the starting point. Pick your moment and ask.
- Be very clear about what you think you are worth—and why. If you have worked harder, achieved more, produced more, gotten better results, you are entitled to say so and ask for compensation.
- Don't bargain just for money—always take into account cars, pensions, vacation entitlements, responsibility, working environment and space, staffing, whatever it is you want.
- If you do get turned down, always find out why and what it is you could do to get what you ask for.
- Return after putting right whatever was wrong in the previous point.
- Remain calm at all times.
- Never compare yourself with anyone else. You are unique, and there is no comparison.

---

[24] Check out *How to Get a Pay Rise, a Bonus, or Promotion, or Whatever It Is You Want* by Ros Jay (Prentice Hall 2001) if you want the definitive guide.

- Never threaten to leave. Leave if you don't get what you want, but no histrionics or threats or bullying. They might just call your bluff, and if they do give into your tantrums, you'll never respect them afterward.

If they say you can't have what you want, find out what it is you have to do; do it and return. Then they can't say no, can they? Getting more money—or anything else—is a matter of negotiating. Those who are good negotiators get more. It's as simple as that. Brush up on your negotiating skills (*see Rule 31*), and don't moan if you don't get what you want. Work harder and go back again.

Don't Follow the Same Route as Everyone Else

Obviously, you can follow whatever route you want, but you might end up in the same place as a lot of other people. If that is a good place, you'll have to share a lot. And if it's a bad place, why be there at all?

Being creative is a brilliant way to make money. Look at all the best moneymakers, and one of the things they share is the ability to be one step ahead, to think creatively (out of the box if you like), and to come up with schemes and ideas that other people haven't thought of. This doesn't mean you have to be reckless or a gambler. It just means thinking differently from other people. But that's the problem most people have. Following the herd is terribly comforting. If it all goes wrong, being in a herd gives a collective feeling of shared grief and the opposite of shared blame. Being a loner and going wrong is a tough cookie to swallow.

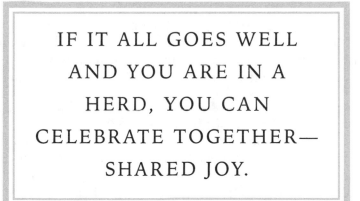

IF IT ALL GOES WELL
AND YOU ARE IN A
HERD, YOU CAN
CELEBRATE TOGETHER—
SHARED JOY.

And the converse is true. If it all goes well and you are in a herd, you can celebrate together—shared joy. It's a bit like being at a football game. It's a good feeling.

You've got to be a person of real courage, confidence, and maturity—not to mention creativity and drive—to stand up and go your own way. You've got to be pretty confident to turn your back on shared joy and shared grief. In the great stock market crash of October 1987, an awful lot of people lost an awful lot of money. Two who didn't, and got out of shares and into cash in August, were the billionaires Kery Packer and Jimmy Goldsmith. Remember, the closer you get to becoming a winner, the less risk you want. And the nearer to losing you get, the more you are inclined to gamble.

I saw a Web site the other day—an investment broker's one— that claimed to show the five most popular stocks and the reasons you should sell them now no matter what your friends, neighbors, or family say. These stocks have been so high for so long that they must crash soon. Sell now and get out ahead of the crowd. I was thinking that real moneymakers wouldn't have been there anyway but would have been out there investing in something none of us had even thought of.

Lots of people invested in ostrich farms. Where are they now? Lots of people invested in worm farms. You bought eggs and turned them into worms, and the big worm farm would buy them back. Loved that one. Yeah, right. Of course, they'll buy all your worms back from you.

One of my sons invested $10 to start his own giant snail business. He bought two giant snails to breed with. (Or should that be from?) He fed and looked after them for about six months when I had to break it to him they were snails out of someone's garden he'd bought. He wasn't alone. Loads of kids at his school were sold the same dream. And the same snails.

PART IV

STAYING
WEALTHY

Now that you've got it, you don't want to let it go, so the next section is how to hang on to it after you get it (assuming you now know to avoid the giant snail scams and the ostrich farms). You'll learn how to preserve, protect, enjoy, and maintain it. After all, when you've finally got it, you don't want to waste it, squander it, throw it away, or give it to me. Actually, the last one isn't true. You can if you really want to.

There are endless Web sites all offering to look after your money for you. Ignore them all. They usually say something like: *Start Your Own Wealth Freedom Journey Today—No Time To Lose*! All you have to do is sign up for a newsletter and buy a get-rich-quick book right away. They promise to make you a millionaire within three to five years.

Perhaps, you should ask for a refund on this book, because I promise you nothing beyond hard work, dedication, focus, creativity, standing out from the crowd, forward planning, and the honest sweat of your brow. Gosh. No promises there at all.

Shop for Quality

My lovely wife taught me this one—credit where it is due. When we met, I was a great one for finding a bargain—two chickens for the price of one at the supermarket, that sort of thing. She, on the other hand, bought less (I never did do anything with that other chicken) but bought quality. So, I would cook a thin and sick-looking chicken and drink it with cheap white wine, and she would provide lobster and champagne. You can see why I fell for her.

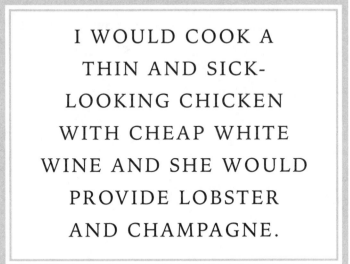

I WOULD COOK A THIN AND SICK-LOOKING CHICKEN WITH CHEAP WHITE WINE AND SHE WOULD PROVIDE LOBSTER AND CHAMPAGNE.

I bought five cheap T-shirts in a pack, and she bought one immaculate T-shirt of much better quality. Now, her stuff

- Lasted longer.
- Washed better.
- Looked better with age.
- Kept its color better.
- Kept its shape better.
- Said more about her in a positive way.
- Took less maintenance. (I drove a cheap car that was always breaking down, and I missed meetings, etc. She drove a better car and always arrived looking calm and immaculate.)

She taught me that the money I was spending, although less, was being wasted because I had to replace stuff much more often. I was throwing money away and looking cheap at that.

Shopping for quality rather than price was a hard lesson to learn. I had to discard all those money myths from my childhood:

- Don't spend more than you need to.
- No one needs to look that expensive.
- It is somehow wrong to spend money on yourself.
- It is somehow better to get a bargain than to buy quality.

Shopping for quality says masses about the way you live, the way you conduct yourself and your business. It says quality to others who will adjust the way they treat you. It also saves you money in the long run—cheap can often be a false economy.

Check the Small Print

I could write you a contract promising you a cast-iron, no get-out clauses, guaranteed, money back without quibbles, cross my heart and hope to die in a cellar full of rats sort of thing that would stand up in a court of law and withstand any scrutiny you cared to put it under. What am I selling? It doesn't matter. Small print can cost you dearly. Check it carefully.

> ## SMALL PRINT CAN COST YOU DEARLY. CHECK IT CAREFULLY.

I love the sort of small print classics, such as taking shoes back that don't fit only to be told they can't be refunded if they have left the store. Or the small print on medications that say they can make you sick and you can't sue. Or the small print on computer software that says you are bound by the agreement if you break the seal on the packaging—and the software can't be tested until it has been run, and you can't run it until you've installed it, and you can't do that until you've broken open the packaging. Agh!

RULE 81

There's a wonderful story of someone who sold his soul to the devil. The devil wanted five years off his life and the person reckoned it was worth it. Oh no! He didn't check the small print. The devil took five years off his life all right—the *first* five years. Agh! Can you imagine what missing the first five years would do to you? And you thought credit card companies were bad?

What do I mean by "checking the small print?" What do you actually have to do? Three basic things:

- Obviously check that it covers you for what you want.
- Check there are no hidden clauses that will twist the basic meaning of the contract.
- Check for penalty clauses—ones that penalize you for late or nonpayment of anything.

It's a bit like checking the small print on food packaging. If you don't like what's in it, don't buy it. Move on up the aisle and buy organic, green, fresh, unpasteurized, whatever. If there is small print, the hairs on the back of your neck should be rising. There is only one reason for it to be there—to trip you up. Move on.

Don't Spend It Before You've Got It

Gosh, this is a hard one for me. I have to admit I find this one of the most difficult to take on board.

How am I to learn this one? Any tips? I know I should:

- Budget for today and only for today. If I don't have it, I don't spend it.
- Ignore what I think or know is coming in the future.
- Put loads aside for taxes—no, even more than that.
- No loans, overdrafts, no borrowings of any sort, so I won't be tempted to use future income to pay off debts run up today—or the reverse, run up debts today knowing that income from the future can be used to pay them off (very naughty).

The downside of spending future income is

- The income may not materialize or may be less than you thought. (Counting chickens that never hatch.)
- The bubble has to burst somewhere, and if you are always spending in advance, you will get caught one day.
- It encourages sloppy financial planning.
- Whatever you bought will have long lost its appeal or wear out, get broken, or even be completely forgotten.
- You lose touch with reality—the future isn't real until it becomes today—and, as such, you can overspend only too easily.

I guess I need a four-point plan:

1 Question whether I need a particular thing today or could wait until later to buy it—a useful ploy because after the "blood lust" has worn off, the appeal often wears off, too.

2 Question whether it is worth it. Obviously, if you're buying today against tomorrow's income, you will incur interest—so is it worth the extra?

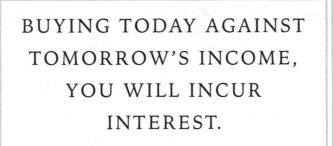

BUYING TODAY AGAINST TOMORROW'S INCOME, YOU WILL INCUR INTEREST.

3 Question the risk factor. If I commit myself today, what if my circumstances change and I need that future income for other purposes?

4 Question that if I spend today, I might not have income for a really exciting spend that might come up—better to keep it just in case.

Follow this with me, and it should reduce our credit card balances considerably.

Put Something Aside for Your Old Age— No, More Than That!

When you realize you are speeding along fast in the outside lane of the age highway and can see less road ahead than there used to be, you should be keen to be sure that if you do stop earning, you will still be able to afford the level of style, luxury, and comfort you now enjoy or want to enjoy.

> IF YOU DO STOP EARNING, YOU WILL STILL BE ABLE TO AFFORD THE LEVEL OF STYLE, LUXURY, AND COMFORT YOU NOW ENJOY OR WANT TO ENJOY.

There are some good reasons why you should put aside money for your old age:

- You can't rely on the government any more.
- If you don't save for yourself, then you may have to rely on the kindness of strangers—or family, which might be worse.
- If you have no old-age plan, you may lose control of your level of comfort, style, and luxury.
- You will lose control of your financial freedom.

- You may lose control of bodily functions and will need money to take care of medical bills.

- As you age, you do slow down, and working as hard as you are now will be impossible.

- You also don't want to *have to* always work hard (though you may choose to). For most of us, there is a time for sitting in the sunshine, and if it isn't when you're old, then when is it?

So why haven't we put something aside already? Well, when we are young, it's hard to envision a time when we won't be. So we don't need to prepare for it. Also, we are too busy having a good time to think about such things. And we are too busy looking after other members of our family to have much time to think about ourselves. Add to that, we are mortgaged up to the hilt, and work is hard enough. Plus, we haven't entered our earning boom period of our fifties, so we don't have lump sums to salt away.

So, if we are going to put something aside, perhaps we need a few guidelines:

- It's never too late to start, but the earlier you do it, the less it will hurt. Prioritize spending—list what you are going to spend on, and see if "the future" is there. If it isn't, put it there, and make it top of the list ahead of that new boat or trip to Paris.

- If you haven't saved much by your fifties, put in a lump sum to seed your retirement plan.[25]

- Get your finances in order and curb waste—spend it instead on your plan.

- If you don't have a pension, make sure you have something that will fund your retirement/later years (property to sell? shares to cash in?) and that it will be sufficient.

- Always think high interest, and move money around to get the best out of it.

- Trade down property as you get older and your needs get smaller. After the kids have left home, you don't need so much space, so invest the profits and downsize.

---

[25] God, don't ever "retire"—you'll drop down dead immediately if you do that!

Put Something Aside for Emergencies/ Rainy Days—the Contingency Fund

As well as saving for your old age, you'll always need to have a contingency fund. I can't give you a definitive list of emergencies, but here's a few to get you thinking. Don't have nightmares now:

- Accidents—motoring, industrial, work-related.
- Illnesses.
- Sudden legal problems—like being sued or arrested wrongly.
- Land disputes—very expensive indeed.
- Problems with children—don't start me off, there are too many to list here, including drugs, unwanted pregnancies, trouble with police, traveling, illnesses, travel problems. (It's expensive to get them back from Thailand when they run out of money and/or enthusiasm.)
- Acts of God—floods, earthquakes, tsunami, droughts, forest fire, pestilence (whatever that is).
- Sudden unemployment.
- Sudden liquidation of your company.
- Recession.

So, how much to put aside, and where do we put it? Well, the wise move is to put aside enough to keep you going in the same style as you live now for three to six months without having to even think about money for that period. Roughly half your annual income if you like. Obviously, if you get completely wiped out in a tsunami or forest fire, you'll be insured and will be able to collect, but you will need something to tide you over. Medical bills can also be covered by insurance.

So, where to keep it? Most people keep it as a savings account—high interest, of course, but instant access. I've noticed the shrewd rich ones keep a safety deposit box with cash for emergencies as well. Always handy in desperate times.

You only have to look at humanitarian disasters to realize how quickly money runs out and how conventional sources become desperately difficult to access. Surviving the storms of Louisiana was bad enough for most people, but it was a great leveller because no one could access the banks because they, too, were under 10 feet of water. Money quickly becomes a useless currency—food and water become the priorities then (and guns, I believe, but I don't want to go there).

You might choose to take out sizeable insurance policies to help alleviate the problems that sudden emergencies can cause.... Alternatively, you might prefer to squirrel away an emergency fund in a highly liquid account (easy quick access), such as a savings account or money market account (which pays higher interest rates). But, as usual, take detailed advice from a proper financial expert—not me.

> # I'VE NOTICED THE SHREWD RICH ONES KEEP A SAFETY DEPOSIT BOX WITH CASH FOR EMERGENCIES AS WELL.

You Paid What for It? How to Shop Around

I know I said shop for quality, and I do really believe that, but I don't believe in throwing your money away on expensive stuff that could be bought more cheaply from another source. For instance, a dear friend was recently buying a very expensive car, a wonderful car. I was most jealous. I was so jealous I broke all my own rules and asked him what he was paying for it. I couldn't believe my ears. "You're paying what for it?!"

He said he could afford it—as indeed he most certainly can. But it was the principle of the thing. "You can get it a lot cheaper here, here, or here," I suggested. "Yes," he replied, "but then I would have to get up off my butt and do something instead of just reaching for the phone."

I offered to buy it for him at the cheaper location and then sell it to him and split the difference. But he was having none of it. He explained he had earned his money so that he could stay on the sofa and lift a phone and have the world brought to him, delivered with the minimum of effort. That was what he thought great wealth was all about.

Now, unlike my friend, the sensible rich don't just throw money away because they can. Instead, they

- Always get at least three quotes for work being done and don't just accept the first quote they get.
- Shop around to make sure they aren't wasting their money.
- Are cautious about spending if they have had to work hard for their money. They aren't miserly, just cautious and selective and discriminating.

There is an old Russian saying that spending is quick but earning long. That's true. We can offload the work of years in a few moments. We have to be prudent when it comes to spending. I don't mean to deny ourselves anything—God forbid I should recommend that. But instead, just be a bit cautious and don't go throwing money away needlessly.

> ## JUST BE A BIT CAUTIOUS AND DON'T GO THROWING MONEY AWAY NEEDLESSLY.

I think wise spending is something we should be teaching our kids from a very early age. They are all too often persuaded by advertising that if something is brightly colored, noisy, messy, or in some way repugnant to parents, it must be a good thing. And they rush home and strip off all those wrappings, and disappointment sets in so very quickly. Teach 'em young.

As for you, time to discover for yourself the joy of getting value for money in everything you buy (if you haven't already). The Internet makes it all terribly easy to compare prices and shop around and be sure you aren't paying more than you have to for anything. Use it.

Never Borrow Money from Friends or Family (but You Can Allow Them to Invest)

I think we might need to have a quick recap of what friends and family are there for—and what you are there for, for them as well. Friends are for

- Caring
- Loving
- Supporting
- Nurturing
- Helping
- Advising—and getting advice from
- Comforting
- Having fun with
- Sharing

Nowhere in that list does it mention:

- Borrowing from
- Stealing from
- Conning

Put simply, it is very bad manners to borrow from friends and family. It sets up too many issues and agendas. It causes resentments, recriminations, and suspicions. It jeopardizes relationships that are important. Don't do it.

IT IS VERY BAD
MANNERS TO BORROW
FROM FRIENDS
AND FAMILY.

Besides which, friends and family aren't proper sources of loans, because they aren't licensed for it. I'm not talking here of the odd $20 to get a round of drinks in, but significantly large amounts—how much that is will depend on your circumstances. You do need to be licensed to be a credit broker (no, seriously), and if you borrow from friends (or conversely lend to the same), you have no legal recourse if it all goes wrong—and it will, as sure as eggs are eggs.

I know technically you could get proper agreements drawn up and all that, but even then, and even if they are charging you the proper interest rates, it's dangerous. If you fail to pay them back—due to circumstances beyond your control, of course—you risk losing their friendship, which, of course, would mean much more to you than the loan would in the first place.

The only exception to this is if family and friends want to invest in, say, a business you are starting, and they fully understand that, like any investment, they may not see a return, and all the usual risks apply. (*See Rule 90* for more on this.) What you can't afford is for it to cause a rift if things don't work out. Family and friends are too important for that.

Don't Surrender Equity

This is a Rule for anybody who runs a company, or who is a freelancer and is thinking of setting himself up as a sole trader business. Essentially, the point is not to give away bits of you or your company.

The aim of the exercise is to preserve wealth, so don't surrender equity (shares or a stake in your company), or you'll be paying someone a share of your hard work, time, and energy. Better to give him money, even if it is with interest, rather than a share of you.

In a later Rule on spending your money, I'll tell you to ask for equity, but that's different—that's you as a lender of money. The shoe is on the other bank account then, so different rules apply.

There is a misconception that having total control of one's business is a bad thing, and many business advisers will advocate giving away equity as a good thing. But I have noticed that the really successful wealthy don't do this. They hang on to every bit they've got. They may borrow and take out loans and run up overdrafts, but they don't give away equity.

Advisers will suggest steering clear of a bank loan because the bank can close down your business so quickly. A business angel will lend money instead, but he will demand equity.

If you do have to surrender equity, make sure you swap it for

- Business skills and acumen
- Hands-on directorships

- A freedom-from-hassle agreement so that you can run the business the way you want
- A realistic percentage so you don't give away too much
- A buy-back clause so you can buy back the equity for cash at a later stage when you are cash rich

I run a company and have some shareholders, but the shares they hold don't give them voting rights. So, although they do get some equity, they don't get control, and, in fact, the shares were given as a reward for advice rather than money I borrowed.

> # NEVER GIVE AWAY
> # VOTING SHARES TO
> # ANYONE.

Only take money into your business from people who have experience in your business and understand its ebbs and flows and industry-related problems. And remember, never give away voting shares to anyone.

Know When to Stop

"What?" I can hear a gasp of surprise. "Know when to stop? Didn't you say earlier that you shouldn't rest on your laurels or they will wilt?" Yes, I did, but that was when you were starting to get results, not when you'd done really well and were wealthier than you thought you ever would be. Look, there has to come a time when enough is enough. There has to come a time when you want to

- Spend more time with your family
- Enjoy your life
- Have fun
- Go travel
- Get the work/life balance tipped a bit in favor of the life
- Use your time to pass on what you have learned to others

> LOOK, THERE HAS TO
> COME A TIME WHEN
> ENOUGH IS ENOUGH.

Of course, you might do all of these without giving up the gaining wealth ideal. It is the focus that stops, perhaps. Being driven to gain prosperity is a good thing; but once gained, you should return to the fold, so to speak. I am always impressed by people like Bill Gates, who decided to retire from his work to run his charitable foundation. In his case, he probably didn't need and couldn't spend or count any more money than he already had/has, and it's probably accumulating faster each day than he can count. He's probably living on the interest on the interest on the interest on the interest....

And I see his close second in the wealth stakes; Warren Buffet, is doing the same—and actually contributing to Bill's foundation.[26] I know these boys are playing around with sums well into the billions, but their hearts are in the right place. These sorts of people are where this rule comes from. Others doing the same include Thomas Monaghan, the Domino Pizza founder, who is reputed to have given away over a billion dollars and founded Ave Maria University.

You're thinking that you aren't anywhere in the same league. No, but you can still have an end game strategy whereby you build an "enough is enough" clause into your plan. Otherwise, where do you stop? How much is enough? Where do you draw the line? There is an Arab saying: *"If you have much, give of your wealth; if you have little, give of your heart."* So, when you get a lot, give some of it away—we'll speak more of this in a moment.

I'm not going to browbeat you about giving to charity, but I am suggesting that knowing when you've got enough money is important. I know there is an expression that you can't have too much of a good thing, but focusing on prosperity is only one part of a rich and varied life, and you can be too dedicated.

---

[26] Sorry, it is actually called the Bill and Melinda Gates Foundation – BMGF – sounds like something from a story by Roald Dahl.

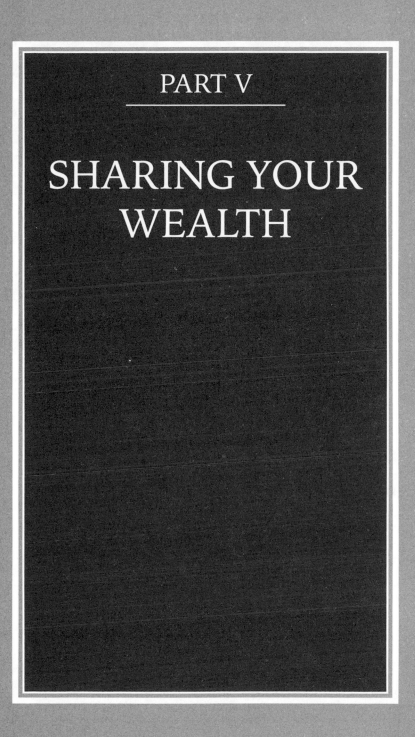

PART V

SHARING YOUR WEALTH

When you've worked hard to earn your wealth, it does seem a bit unfair to share it. But if you don't, you run the risk of your hardworking outstretched hand turning into an arthritic grasping claw. Money can be earned, grown, guarded, fought over, used well, used badly, won, lost, buried, invested, given away, bought back, exchanged, and divided up. But the nicest thing to do with it is surely to share it.

I'm not talking do-gooding here. I'm talking sharing because sharing is a kind thing to do. It won't buy you a ticket into heaven, but it will help others. I know you've worked hard, grafted, and burned the midnight oil to get to where you are today, and why should you give it away to those who are lazy, less focused, indulgent, or plain liberty-takers? Yep, good point. But I'm talking here about the less well off, the unfortunate, the weak, the needy, and the deserving.

Wealth is a bit like a beautiful painting. Sure, you can hang it in your study and only you get to look at it. But you can also share it and let others look as well. Ah, but you'll say wealth decreases if we share it. Does it? Does it really? I doubt it somehow. I think for every penny you give away—or share with someone less able to gain prosperity—you double its value. Maybe not in hard cash, but in other ways.

As I say, I don't want to browbeat you. It's just I've noticed that the really successful, happy rich people do feel at ease sharing their wealth, and that is a lesson for all of us.

Use Your Wealth Wisely

I read of a nice couple the other day—both rock musicians—who had bought a big house in the countryside with nine acres and were settling down to raise kids, and I thought that was a good investment because it provides

- A stable place to bring up kids
- A nice place to live in the sense of peace and quiet with no city pollution
- A friendly place for the children to grow up with neighbors looking out for them
- A sound investment in history and heritage

On the other hand, I read in the same paper of a fashion model who was in the news a lot because of her drug habit. An expensive habit, I have no doubt. I guess you can see where my interests lie from these two snippets gleamed from the newspaper. One is a sound and wise investment, and the other is just self-indulgent trouble that lends nothing to the wisdom of wealth.

I'm not a party pooper, but I have noticed that those who handle their wealth sensibly, share it, and are generous with their time and money get back a whole lot more than those who squander, misuse, indulge, and generally behave as if their wealth gives them a licence to show off. Enough moralizing and preaching. I did promise not to. But these are genuine observations, and I'm sure you've made similar observations. Those who abuse their wealth don't tend to stay wealthy for long. Here are a few questions regarding our wealth and how wisely we might handle it:

- Why did we get wealthy in the first place?
- What is the best use of wealth?
- What are our long-term goals and expectations for our wealth?
- What do we think our wealth will bring us?
- What could we do with our wealth that would be beneficial to others?
- What sort of world do we want?
- How do we and our wealth wish to be seen?
- What will they say about us after we've gone?
- What legacy will we leave behind?

> THOSE WHO ABUSE
> THEIR WEALTH DON'T
> TEND TO STAY WEALTHY
> FOR LONG.

I think the best use of wealth is to teach children how to earn it, invest it, save it, and spend it wisely. As we all get more and more affluent, there is a real need to introduce some element of monetary discussion into the curriculum. Children need to learn about tax, insurance, and spending, and all the stuff we never got taught and have had to learn the hard way as we went along. Mind you, I would also make sure every child could read and write before they left school and could drive a car.

Never Lend Money to Friends or Family Unless You Are Prepared to Write It Off

Can you share your wealth with family and friends? Yes, but if you want to retain your sanity, I would strongly suggest you don't lend anyone any money unless, mentally, you are prepared to write it off. That way when they don't repay you—and I bet they won't—you'll feel just fine about it. If you expect them to repay you and they don't, imagine how hurt and let down you are going to feel.

I know. I have sons. But my money is for them as much as it is for me, so we play this game of them asking for a loan and my giving it to them. Sometimes, they pay it back and I am pleasantly surprised, but sometimes, they don't and I write it off, and that's fine, too. (I really hope they don't read this, or I'll be cornered in my own home like a rat.)

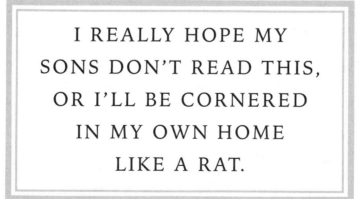

I REALLY HOPE MY
SONS DON'T READ THIS,
OR I'LL BE CORNERED
IN MY OWN HOME
LIKE A RAT.

RULE 90

I value my kids and their relationship with me, and I wouldn't want to fall out with them over something as squalid as money when there are so many better things to fall out with them over anyway.

If you do lend money to friends and don't get it back, you lose more than just the money—you lose the friendship as well. They feel embarrassed because they aren't repaying you and thus don't come round to see you. You feel grieved and don't invite them because of it. Result: end of friendship.

Write it off, though, and you'll still be happy to see them and they'll quickly forget the embarrassment and regard you as one of a kind.

Of course, you don't have to do either. You can just say no. (*See Rule 93.*) Or you could just give them money. (*See Rule 94.*)

I've been reading an advice blog on the web about a young man who lent his roommate at college $350—not a huge amount—but the repayment never materialized. He had asked various friends first if they had ever lent his roommate money, and they said he had paid them back. Now he has, of course, fallen out big time with his roommate—despite offering him the option of repayment terms at $50 a month. Worse still, he has fallen out with all his other friends because they "approved" the loan in his eyes.

The advice was to take the friend to court, but I figure he won't see the money anyway and will incur a lot of legal expense into the bargain. Better to chalk it up to experience and walk away whistling. I know, for him, it is a lot of money, but any decent education doesn't come cheap. The discussion did go on into his rights to "seize" his roommate's possessions and so on. I still say walk away whistling, and don't ever do it again.

RULE 91

Don't Lend; Take Equities

If you are asked for a loan by somebody for a specific project such as starting a company or expanding one, there are a variety of answers including

- No
- Yes
- Yes, but
- Yes, on the condition that
- Yes, with equity
- Yes, with a convertible loan

Obviously "no" can cause offense. (*See Rule 93*.) "Yes" is a no-no, if you see what I mean. Lending friends and family money isn't good unless you are prepared to write it off (*see Rule 90*), and generally, people who want big loans aren't that close or they'd know you better.

This leaves us with the last three—conditions, equity, or convertible? There may be others, of course.

Conditions. A fool's game if you ask me. On the condition you repay me when you've made your fortune. Hmm. On the condition you don't do anything silly with this. Hmm. On the condition you only use this for the good of mankind. Hmm. Conditions are so tricky, but there are many who'll ask for them—"If you would just be so good as to lend me this, I promise to ... blah blah." Yeah, right.

Equity. Better. You don't lend; you offer to buy a share in whatever project it is. If it is successful, you recoup with interest. If it fails, you shouldn't have been lending—or buying into it—in the first place. More the fool you. The trouble with equity is that it's often black and white, hit or miss. You get your money back if the project is successful—and perhaps that should be *when* the project is successful.

Convertible. Much better. You lend as a proper loan with repayment details all worked out legally so that it is a binding loan. But if the project is successful—it should be or you shouldn't be lending in the first place—you convert the loan into equity. This way, you get your money back plus a big share of the profits. It sort of makes lending seem worthwhile.

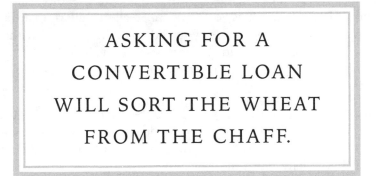

ASKING FOR A CONVERTIBLE LOAN WILL SORT THE WHEAT FROM THE CHAFF.

If approached for a loan, asking for a convertible loan will sort the wheat from the chaff, the serious from the not so serious. It makes the serious stand up and be counted. If the project then fails, you get your money back—in theory at least. Obviously, if the project fails, there may not be any money, but you will have secured it against the borrower's property, of course. (I know I said never to do that, but that was advice for you as a borrower. As a lender, always make sure you do.) I even do this with my children if tempted to lend them any money for big items like cars and houses. Yes, you can have the money, but I want to own a share, so you can't sell it if you get bored or restless or whatever without my permission. Amazing how often they back off when they know I'll be their partner. And I also then know that they did buy the item rather than something they'd rather not tell me about.

You Really, Really Can't Take It with You

I know there's a saying—whoever has the most toys at the end wins. But you really can't take it with you, and you can't buy anything with it when you go—no tickets into heaven, no indulgences, no get-out-of-hell free cards. When you go, you go alone and with nothing, just as you came in. So all that effort, in a way, is wasted. Unless, of course, you did something useful with it when you had it and had the ability to do it. Left drooling in some old folks' home isn't the time or place to start being philanthropic, is it?

Not getting rid of it is known as *wealth bondage*—being tied so tightly to your money that you really do try to take it with you— and that really is kinky. Sure, you can leave it to your kids, but you should have given most of it away long before you bite the bullet, or you'll be leaving a massive tax liability for someone down the line.

> ## NOT GETTING RID OF YOUR MONEY IS KNOWN AS WEALTH BONDAGE.

Whatever you decide to do, take the proper advice—nothing grates so much as a poorly thought-out will and lots of tax after you've gone.

You can, of course, insure against tax liabilities after you've gone. You have to calculate what you think your tax liability is likely to be and then set up a whole-of-life insurance policy to cover it. The policy has to be written into a trust to ensure the proceeds from the policy aren't included with your estate, but for heaven's sake, be careful on placing anything in trust, because if you use the wrong one, you can make things even worse. Also, legislation can change.

Gosh, I'm not a financial adviser (except on a behavioral level—you need somebody else for the nitty-gritty-which-investment-is-best-for-me detail), but it seems to make sense to have all this tied up before you go. And, of course, you can leave the lot to your spouse, and then she doesn't have to pay death taxes, but her tax bill is going to be high when she goes, so you are only delaying rather than offsetting. You can establish a trust to ensure that both the husband and wife's inheritance rights are fully utilized—but again, be very careful using a trust.

I was reading about the Dalai Lama's wealth the other day. He gets paid the equivalent of around 38 cents a day for expenses, owns two robes—one on and one in the wash—and his only indulgence is a new watchstrap every now and again. (I did wonder if he bought leather ones.) And yet, he is the head of an entire country—albeit one in exile. Now that is cool in my book.

Know When/How to Say No—and Yes

Now that you've made some money, there will be those who see you as

- A target—easy pickings.
- Owing them something—after all, they have known you for years.
- Worth taking a chance on—you never know.
- A genuine source of low-interest loans or free gifts—and so much easier than preparing a proper business plan and going to the bank.

I'm not saying you will always get the outstretched hand. In fact, some requests will be cloaked in the most attractive brochures of potential investments. So how do you know when to say yes and when to say no? And how to say either?

Saying no to friends and family is easy, in a sense. Right from day one, you make it a policy—and a very easily identifiable one—not to lend to friends and family. (*See Rule 90.*) You never do, so they learn not to ask.

Saying no to business acquaintances is also easy. Just ask them to refer everything to your accountant or business adviser. Say you never make a decision without his input and you can't proceed until he has studied everything in close detail. That puts off the ones who are just arm-round-the-shoulder trying it on. The others might be worth considering if they have genuine plans—in which case, it might be worth having a look.

RULE 93

Know when to say yes or no. Say no if

- Your gut instinct says to say no.
- They haven't done any work on their presentation—if they are lazy at ground zero, it strikes me they'll be lazy right through.
- You have no connection with them—always say no to strangers, basically.

To say yes is fine. To say no is fine. It's your money, and you can do with it what you want. You have to

- Let go of any guilt—this is business.
- Make sure you understand exactly what is being asked for—that's why calling in advisors is always a good idea.
- Keep a closed-door policy to stop yourself from being overwhelmed by requests—make it hard for them to get to you.
- Avoid saying yes because you think it will make people happy—they are emotionally blackmailing you and thus get themselves crossed off the list automatically and without guilt.
- Always be very clear when you are saying "no." No "maybes" or "we'll see" or "I'll have to sleep on that one." Say no and put everyone out of their misery—including you.
- Don't allow yourself to be badgered. Be assertive.
- Stop them in their tracks—a simple "I'd rather you didn't ask me" before they've even gotten started.

Find Ways to Give People Money Without Them Feeling They Are in Your Debt

I love this one. It is such a challenge to give money to people who

- Haven't asked for it
- Need it
- Deserve it
- Will use it wisely/well

And the challenge is to get them to accept it without feeling indebted to you, beholden, grudging, guilty, whatever. This is one of those rules we all ought to practice no matter how much money we have. I bet you get to start as soon as you become a parent and give your kids big money for cars and things. They are always saying, "I'll pay you back," and you know they won't. But if you can give them money without all that stuff being attached to it, you are doing well.

> IF YOU CAN GIVE PEOPLE MONEY WITHOUT ALL THAT STUFF BEING ATTACHED TO IT, YOU ARE DOING WELL.

There are a variety of tips to help you give your money away without the recipients feeling guilty or you feeling embarrassed:

- The "You might win the lottery one day" approach. This is a good one, because it implies that there, but for a bit of luck, you go. All they've got to do is be as lucky as you, and they'll pay you back.

- The "Fortunes change, and they go down as well as up" approach. Basically, what you are saying is that you are flush at the moment, but that might not always be the case, and when your fortunes go down, they can help you out.

- The "I like my friends to be happy" approach. How can I be happy when I see my friends in misery/trouble/debt/whatever? If you aren't happy, then I can't be, so I'll help myself to become happy by helping you to become happy. How can anyone refuse?

- This is the "Why shouldn't I help my friends?" approach—a subset of the one above but still valuable and useful. Look, it's what friends are for. You've helped me out in the past/are helping me by/have always offered help anyway, so why can't I do the same for you?

- The "Help me out here—I've got a tax problem" approach. Look, if I can offload some of this cash, I can alleviate my tax burden, so can you help me by taking some? I would be ever so grateful.

- The "Taxman will only get it after I'm dead" approach. So, can I give it to you now and see the pleasure it'll bring you rather than your grieving and moping after I've gone?

- Help them with a housing upgrade by taking equity in the new house. They pay nothing until they snuff it, at which point, your investment will probably show better appreciation than the interest rate it would have earned on deposit. And if it doesn't, so what? Profit was never the point anyway, but they can feel happy about it.

I'm sure if you put your mind to it, there will be many more you can come up with. Hey, this one is fun. You get to help others, give loads away, share your wealth, and be creative all at the same time.

Don't Over-Protect Your Children from the Valuable Experience of Poverty

Look, if you're about to ask your parents for a really big loan (gift?), then you'd better buy up every copy of this book you can and burn them, because you're not going to like what I have to say next.

Parents, if you are reading this, then don't give your kids that loan (gift). It is okay not to pamper them, to make them learn the value of money, to make them treat money with respect right from the word go. Just because you have lots, doesn't mean they are entitled to stand there with their hand out right from the day they get out of diapers.

> ## A MONTHLY ALLOWANCE IS ALWAYS A GOOD IDEA.

I'm the world's worst at this one, but I am learning. There are various ways you can go from being utterly mean and not giving them a cent to being overly generous and giving them every-thing. Now, I am going to talk about setting budgets for children and setting up trust funds for them.

A monthly allowance is always a good idea because they then have to live within their means. It teaches them to budget and to scrimp and save at the end of the month—or halfway through it in most cases. When they first go off to college is probably the best time to do this because they are also learning a whole new batch of things about being grown up—sex, drugs, staying out late, wrong sort of friends, binge drinking. Learning to balance their own books at the same time is good for them.

You can set aside lump sums for them, as well, so they can buy a house, business, decent car. If you administer it, then they can't blow it on a plasma TV or a $600 designer handbag, but spend it on only a sensible thing that they have to explain to you in some detail. And, of course, you can give them a trust fund for when you have shuffled off. Or, of course, let them have such a fund when they are of an age sensible enough to enjoy it without it diverting them from their education. I would give it to them after it would make any real difference to them—in effect, after they have started to earn their own money in worthwhile amounts.

And, for goodness' sake, don't ever tell them they are getting a lump sum aged 25 or whatever you decide. Nothing demotivates kids more than thinking they're coming into money. They'll think they don't have to make an effort. Let them think they'll always be poor, and watch them go.

How do you set a good allowance figure? Only you can work it out for your kids, and it obviously varies depending on age, but once they reach their teens, it's as well to thrash it out with them—a process sometimes of painful discussion. But make them argue every penny and justify it. It'll make them value it when they get to spend it.

Know How to Choose Charities/Good Causes

When you have some money, you get inundated with requests to give to charities. I'm not talking about the emotional blackmail ones we all get through the mail—these three pennies could pay for food for an entire family forever and a rainforest and sight for all the blind people in the world, and all you have to do is send them back with whatever you can afford. Oh, the guilt when you spend those three pennies—not!

I'm talking about big charitable donations, supporting a particular cause, supporting a particular person. I've always had my doubts—and this is entirely subjective, entirely personal—about supporting a penguin or endangered fish or threatened albatross. How do you know which is yours? In the zoo, you can at least go and have a look at your own saved pet, but in the wild, it is so much more difficult.

> I'VE ALWAYS HAD MY
> DOUBTS—AND THIS IS
> ENTIRELY SUBJECTIVE,
> ENTIRELY PERSONAL—
> ABOUT SUPPORTING
> A PENGUIN.

Anyway, here are a few tips for choosing a good charity—a good one for you:

- Decide what is important to you—the planet, saving whales, small children, the poor, cancer research.
- Work out what you want to do—just give money, get involved, be an adviser, raise funds. (I've always wanted to drive one of those inflatables for Greenpeace; I just think those boats are so cool.)
- Check out charities you might think suitable on the Internet and see if your ideals fit in with theirs.
- Check out the charities themselves—financial statements, accounts, brochures, campaign information, membership, mission statements.
- Trust your gut feelings.

I reject any charities that directly approach me. It's not because it makes me cross, but it's my way of weeding out the ones I don't want to support. I have my own mission statements when it comes to charity giving, and not being approached is part of that. I also like charities that set out to help directly instead of merely churning out aid—teaching villagers to fish and all that. I also support only small charities because I figure they need it more.

And I will support only small charities that are doing things that seem attainable. I figure feeding the poor of the world requires a bottomless pit. It's not that it isn't a decent objective, but it's one I find too remote. I can relate to one that seeks to provide fresh water for a particular village, or one that provides a breakfast for an inner-city schoolkid.[27]

---

[27] www.magicbreakfast.co.uk is something I *can* get my head round.

Spend Your Own Money, Because No One Will Spend It as Wisely as You

What! Surely, we all spend our own money? No, we don't. As we get richer, the need to have others spend it for us grows stronger. Believe me, it becomes a real risk to hand things over and lose value and wealth because of it. It is so easy to figure that because we are busy and someone offers, our money is a good thing to hand over.

I have noticed that the successful rich don't hand over anything; they continue paying attention to detail all the time. Obviously, there might come a time to hand over as we grow too old to administer our own affairs, but until then, give up nothing.

> I HAVE NOTICED THAT
> THE SUCCESSFUL RICH
> DON'T HAND OVER
> ANYTHING.

Examples? Of course. I have a friend who has considerable wealth and who is happy to hand over his spending to anyone around him who offers to do it for him. His gardener buys all his equipment, including mowers and chain saws and the like. Top of the range? I should say. This gardener is driving around on mowers that are the gardening equivalent of a Rolls Royce. My friend just signs the checks, and the gardener is laughing all the way to the tool shed. My friend also pays caterers to come in and organize meals every time he wants to entertain. Again, he signs the check, and the caterers supply him with a complete dinner party.

Ah, but I hear you say, "So what? He can afford it." Yes, indeed he can, but he is also

- Being ripped off repeatedly.
- Not getting good value for money.
- Slowly losing control over his own financial affairs.
- Losing the respect of his employees and hired service companies who see him as a bit of a joke—too much money and not enough sense. (It would be all right if he was aristocracy, because you expect it of them, but he is a self-made rich person.)

He's the same when it comes to buying a new car. He just rings up the showroom, and they deliver what he wants. Trouble is, they frequently deliver what they've had sitting in their show-rooms for too long and can't sell. Ask him about the pink Bentley he bought that no one else was going to touch in a mil-lion years. I tease him and ask him if the showroom had a big glass office where they could sit and see him coming.

You've got to retain control of your own spending if you want to retain control over your finances—and dignity. No pink Bentleys for you. Don't hand out credit cards. Don't give anyone authority to sign personal checks. Don't use a personal shopper. Set people proper budgets. Get them to submit proper proposals for spending. Check the small print. Check everything. Question everything. Stay on top. Stay in control. And if you want my advice—no joint accounts ever. There's no need for it in this day and age.

Take Responsibility Before You Take Advice

This is a follow-up from the previous Rule. If you are going to take advice, you need to know in advance

- What you expect to get.
- Why you are asking.
- Your exact position—if you don't know, how can they advise you of anything?
- What you want to happen next.
- What role they will play in that.
- What action you can take if their advice is wrong/out of date/ harmful.
- What further advice you might need.

And before you can do any of these, you need to take responsibility.

We all start out—or at least I did, and so did most people I've ever talked to about it—somehow expecting that we would end up rich. It was/is an assumed process, sort of by osmosis. As you get older and add years to your life, so in theory you add riches. Then, you wake up one day, and it isn't/is just like that. For me, it wasn't, so I went into hyperdrive to change the situation and am now fabulously wealthy.[28] But it took hard work and tremendous effort. Now, you've made it, it is time to review. Time to take responsibility. Time to take stock. You need to know

- Where you are
- How you got there

---

[28] If you are the tax collector, I was only joking, and/or I've already paid my tax bill.

- What you are worth—both financially and spiritually
- Where you want to go next
- How you expect to get there

When you have answered these questions, you are ready to take advice about your plans. And it doesn't have to be advice of the paid kind, the expert kind, the man-in-a-suit kind, the all serious and heavy kind. Sometimes, advice can come from unlikely sources and unlikely people. Learn to listen. Learn to take in what is *not* being said. Learn to be happy. (Gosh, that's a big one for all of us.)

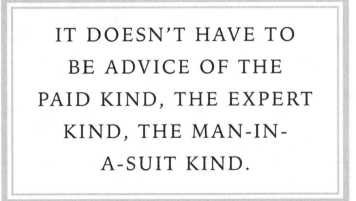

> # IT DOESN'T HAVE TO BE ADVICE OF THE PAID KIND, THE EXPERT KIND, THE MAN-IN-A-SUIT KIND.

The wealthier we become, the easier it appears to be to hand over our affairs (financial ones) to people we think have our best interests at heart or who we assume know what they are doing or are on top of the latest developments and laws. My observation is that (a) they're not and (b) the shrewd wealthy ones don't hand over anything unless they are really, really sure of their advisers. And that's my advice.

Once You've Got It, Don't Flaunt It

Wealth is lovely. Having money is great. Getting rich is a worth-while and enjoyable activity. Buying the pink Bentley is just plain gross, as are a lot of other things that shout *nouveau riche*, over-the-top, flaunting, bling. So tacky. Take lessons in how to handle wealth by all means, but do handle it well.

I read a nice story the other day of a young man who got to stay in a millionaire's mansion—a relative I assume—and when he went to bed, he left the light on. The millionaire popped his head round the door and told him it was wasting money and he should turn it off. He even threatened him with a $1 fine. But instead, he tossed him a $1 bill and turned the light out himself. The kid never forgot the incident and is still turning lights off when he goes to bed or leaves a room to this day. And, he still doesn't know why the reverse psychology worked. As he says, he went from a possible $1 fine to a big windfall. (It was 1953, when a dollar was a lot.)

Be frugal. Be careful with your money. Don't flaunt it. And as you now belong to an exclusive club, could you please observe a few rules:

- No flashy cars
- No castles, ranches, or ranch-style houses—this isn't Dallas, you know
- No bling
- No glitz or showing off
- No impulse spending
- No wild animals as pets

- No buying islands
- No private jets
- No flying all your relatives to a foreign county for a party
- No flying your relatives to a foreign country for your latest trophy wedding
- No huge diamonds—or big jewelery of any sort—it'll only attract the robbers and thieves

Be a discreet, tasteful, refined, cultured, less-is-more, more-is-tacky, quiet sort of rich person. Someone we can all look up to. Someone who will inspire and not cultivate ridicule—they do laugh at those leopard skin trousers, I'm afraid (not that you've got any). Someone who will set a good example to the young, the impressionable, the not so well-off.

We've all seen those who come into money too suddenly and flaunt the fact that they have loads, and we all think, "God, how tacky." I know we shouldn't sit in judgment on others, but I do find my toes curl at…no, I can't say in case you've got one.

Flaunting it creates envy, jealousy (different from envy), criticism, snobbery, condemnation, censure—and all quite rightly. Discretion, on the other hand, encourages respect, admiration, and emulation. Never mention how much you've got, what you are worth, or how much you earn. Ever. If you tell people, half will despise you for not having more, and the other half resent you for having so much. Only reveal such information to your bank manager, and even then, they should have to drag the info from you.

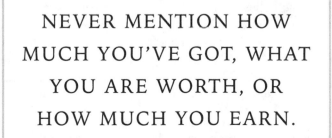

NEVER MENTION HOW MUCH YOU'VE GOT, WHAT YOU ARE WORTH, OR HOW MUCH YOU EARN.

What's Next?
Pacts with the Devil?

It's the last Rule, and I guess we can have some fun. Creating wealth is as varied and different an adventure for each of us as anything else. We can work for it, win the lottery or a poker game (mind you, it would have to be a pretty big one), inherit it, steal it, be awarded it as a prize (Nobel Peace Prize for literature—you do get around $1.3 million.[29] Gulp. Put my name forward at once please, somebody. Or what about the Templeton Prize, which gets you $1.4 million),[30] or find it in the street (lots of examples on the Internet of people finding huge wads of cash), marry into it, you name it. And, of course, if you are really desperate, there is the old pact with the devil—but beware of gotcha clauses.

BEWARE OF GOTCHA CLAUSES.

The Chinese believe, via feng shui, that if you leave your toilet seat up, your money will get flushed away. I wonder if this is a modern invention, because I have no evidence of toilets flushing in China when feng shui was being established in the Taoist eras.

---

[29] 10 million Swedish krona—the actual value changes with fluctuating currency conversion rates.

[30] The Templeton Prize is awarded annually by an international, multifaith panel of judges to a living person of any religious tradition who has made a unique contribution to progress in research or discoveries about spiritual realities.

Then, there are affirmations—you write down the wealth you want and pin it up so you can see it every day and chant it out hundreds of times. Might work. Then, there's writing it down and putting it under your pillow so that you'll dream of where your wealth is buried.

Then, there's the cosmic ordering service—you tell the great cosmic bank how much it owes you, and it repays you immediately. There has got to be a catch there somewhere, knowing banks—they're all the same I reckon.

Then, there are money maps and money boards—you cut up pictures of expensive stuff you can buy and would want and make a sort of scrapbook, but as a board, and look at it a lot, I guess. Might work.

Then, there are crystals—you wear one/sleep with it/carry it around. Certain crystals resonate with the cosmic bank (them again), and it's a sort of rock check, I guess.[31]

Dowsing? You follow divining rods (or bits of bent coat hangers and empty ball-point pens, depending on which books you read) that twitch when you are above buried treasure or a seam of gold or one of those ring-pull things off the top of a beer can. A little like a metal detector, but doesn't need batteries.

I suppose you could buy a racehorse, but it seems so very risky to me. How about painting a masterpiece and hanging onto it until (a) it gets valuable or (b) you get dead? Hoarding fine wines? Could work, but I couldn't resist the temptation, I think.

I am not scoffing at any of these methods. However you intend to gain prosperity, you should get on with it, believe in it, follow it, give 100 percent to it, and not listen to others. Including me. Especially me. Good luck.

Richard Templar

---

[31] Citrine, ruby, and tiger eye are supposed to work, but I figure if you can buy rubies, you don't need the wealth or you're giving it all to the crystal seller, so I suppose it works for him.

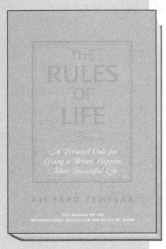

THE RULES OF LIFE
A Personal Code for Living a Better, Happier, More Successful Life

Richard Templar

Some people seem more contented, more fulfilled, more enthusiastic about life...just plain happier. Is it genes? Money? No. It's about the choices they make, the ways they behave, every single day. In *The Rules of Life*, Richard Templar brings together 100 rules that happy, successful people follow: small, simple, common-sense, doable rules that make a powerful difference. Learn personal rules for facing the world more successfully. Learn about interacting with your partner, family, colleagues, friends...and the world. He offers true wisdom on knowing what's important...focusing on changes you really can make... using your intuition...learning from life...staying young...having great dreams and practical plans. Follow The Rules. You'll feel better. You'll be a better friend, partner, parent, human being. Not all at once: one small, simple step at a time. Every day. Starting today.

ISBN 0131743961 ■ ISBN-13 9780131743960 ■ © 2006
240 pp. ■ $16.99 USA ■ $20.99CAN

THE RULES OF MANAGEMENT
A Definitive Code for Managerial Success

Richard Templar

You're smart, talented, competent, responsible. So... they made you a manager. And suddenly, all that good stuff...just ain't enough. You need to know what the greatest managers know: *The Rules of Management*. Here they are. All 100 of 'em. For managing teams. For managing you. Read 'em. Learn 'em. Live 'em. Next thing you know, you'll be looking good. Relaxed. Confident. Assertive. In charge. In control. You'll be building and leading teams that do the impossible, follow you anywhere, and bring passion to work (yes, even at your company). *The Rules of Management*: they're not just rules. They're your blueprint for greatness...and shortcut to the executive suite.

ISBN 013187036X ■ ISBN-13 9780131870369 ■ © 2005
240 pp. ■ $16.95 USA ■ $20.95CAN